HAPPY 60th BIRTHDAY!

HOPE THAT BEING A GRANDPARENT
IS ALL THAT YOU HAVE LOOKED
FORWARD TO.

BASED ON THE JOB YOU DID AS
A PARENT THIS SHOULD BE
EASY.

ENJOY.

Madeline & Seamus

GRANDPARENTHOOD

Other Books by Dr. Ruth K. Westheimer

The Art of Arousal

All in a Lifetime

Dr. Ruth's Encyclopedia of Sex

Dr. Ruth's Guide to Good Sex

Dr. Ruth's Guide for Married Lovers

Dr. Ruth's Guide to Sensuous and Erotic Pleasures

Dr. Ruth's Guide to Safer Sex

Dr. Ruth Talks About Grandparents

Dr. Ruth Talks to Kids

Heavenly Sex: Sex in the Jewish Tradition
  (with Jonathan Mark)

Sex and Morality: Who Is Teaching Our Sex Standards?
  (with Dr. Lou Lieberman)

Surviving Salvation: The Ethiopian Jewish Family in
  Transition *(with Dr. Steven Kaplan)*

Sex for Dummies

The Value of Family

Other Books by Steven Kaplan, Ph.D.

The Beta Israel (Falasha) in Ethiopia

Surviving Salvation: The Ethiopian Jewish Family in
  Transition *(with Dr. Ruth K. Westheimer)*

GRANDPARENTHOOD

DR. RUTH K. WESTHEIMER
AND DR. STEVEN KAPLAN

Routledge

New York and London

Published in 1998 by
Routledge
29 West 35th Street
New York, NY 10001

Printed in Great Britain by
Routledge
11 New Fetter Lane
London EC4P 4EE

10 9 8 7 6 5 4 3 2

LIBRARY OF CONGRESS CATALOGING-IN-PUBLICATION DATA
Westheimer, Ruth K. (Ruth Karola), 1928–
    Grandparenthood / by Ruth K. Westheimer and Steven Kaplan.
        p.   cm.
    Includes bibliographical references.
    ISBN 0-415-91948-7 (cloth).
    1. Grandparenting. 2. Grandparents. I. Kaplan, Steven.
    II. Title.
    HQ759.9.W386   1998
    306.874'5—dc21   98-26073
                                                            CIP

Dedication

I dedicate this book to the memory of my beloved parents and grandparents, who in an indescribable sacrifice sent me, their only child and grandchild, to safety and who perished in concentration camps during World War II.

The set of values, the joie de vivre, and the positive outlook they instilled in me live on in my life and in the new family I have created to carry on their traditions. Sadly, I also dedicate this book to my late husband, Fred, who took so much pride in our family: Miriam Westheimer, Ed.D., and Joel Einleger; Joel Westheimer, Ph.D., and Barbara Leckie, Ph.D.; and the greatest grandchildren on earth, Ari, Leora, and Michal.

—R.W.

To the memory of my grandparents, Simon and Tanya Horowitz and Abraham and Edith Kaplan. And to Albert Owens, my favorite grandmother, with love.

—S.K.

Acknowledgments

Fortunately, my list of people to thank grows with each book—it would take an extra chapter to list them all. So to all of you, a warm thank you! In addition, the following people must be mentioned by name:

Pierre Lehu, my "Minister of Communications," the best that anybody could wish for—a special toast to many more years of cooperation. All of the relatives, cousins, and their families—a hug! I do want to thank the following people for adding so much to my life: Ruth Bachrach, Bill Baker, Rabbi and Mrs. Stephen Berkowitz, Susan Brown, Carlita de Chavez, Hersh Cohen, Esther Coopersmith, Mary Cuadrado, Ph.D., Martin Englisher, Cynthia and Howard Epstein, Gabe and Susie Eram, Steve Friedman, Ellen Goldberg, David Goslin, Ph.D., Vladimir Goussinsky, Michael Greenspan, Amos Grunebaum, M.D., David and Doreen Hermelin, Dennis and Brooke Holt, Elliot Horowitz, Fred Howard, John Jacobs, Richard Kandel, Alfred Kaplan, Helen Singer Kaplan, Michael and Ronnie Kassan, Bonnie Kaye, Richard and Barbara Kendall, Phill and Bonnie Kendall, Harold and Linda Koplewitz, Marga and Bill Kunreuther, Rabbi and Mrs. William LeBeau, Sasha Klein, Cantor and Mrs. Michael Kruk, Joanne Lehu, Esq., Lou Lieberman, Ph.D., John and Ginger Lollos, Sandy Lopater, Jonathan and Ruchy Mark, Dale Ordes, Marga and Michael Miller, Bobby and Vicky Nachamie, Michelle and Linden Nelson, Henry and Sydelle Ostberg, Robert Pinto, Fred and Ann Rosenberg, Colin Rosin, Cliff Rubin, Tim and Tami Satterfield, Simeon and Rose Schreiber, Gangadai (Cindy) Seepersaud, Romie and Blanche Shapiro, Amir Shaviv, John Silberman, John and Marianne Slade, Richard Stein, Rudi Steinbach, Robert Stewart, Hannah Strauss, Malcolm and Barbara Thomson, Gary Tinterow, Mike and Vicky Turek, Mildred Witkin, Ph.D., Greg Willenborg, and Ben Yogada.

A very special bravo, thank you, and gratitude to the superb professionals at Routledge: Colin Jones, Heidi Freund, Sarita Sahni, Shea Settimi, John McHale, and Laura-Ann Robb—I add my voice to all the accolades that Steve heaped upon them. And what a terrific coauthor I have! Thank you!

—R.W.

The subject matter and style of this book mark a significant departure from any of my previous books or articles. Its completion and publication could not have been accomplished without the support of numerous people. First and foremost, I would like to thank Ruth K. Westheimer for her friendship, her generosity, and the faith she demonstrated in choosing me as her collaborator on this book. Colin Jones, the president of Routledge, shared his confidence and took a chance when others in his position might have hesitated. Heidi Freund, our editor, provided much-needed advice and encouragement as the book first took shape, guided it through numerous rough drafts, and provided detailed comments for shaping it into its final form. Sarita Sahni, Shea Settimi, and Laura-Ann Robb dealt efficiently with a variety of technical issues that arose as the book moved toward completion.

The Harry S. Truman Research Institute of the Hebrew University of Jerusalem provided the infrastructure and working conditions necessary for my work, including Internet, e-mail, faxes, and computer facilities. I thank all my colleagues there.

My friends, David Satran, Mindy Milberg, Linda Aronson, Kay K. Shelemay, Hagar Salamon, Rafi Youngman, Rachel Melesa, and Monica Devens, were always enthusiastic in their support for this project and often provided me with insights on families and grandparents.

My mother, Ruth Kaplan, taught me most of what I know about families, both in her daily role as mother and through her own reading and teaching about family systems. My sisters Eva and Judy have repeatedly reminded me that I have their full support in whatever I do, wherever I do it.

During the period when this book was written, my household grew from three members to five, and we became an interfaith, interracial, blended family. That I was able to write this book during this period of change is a tribute to the patience and understanding of Booshun, Yona, Egypt (Denise), and Albert.

—S.K.

Contents

Introduction

The Lord bless thee out of Zion; and see thou
the good of Jerusalem all the days of thy life;
and see thy children's children. Peace be upon Israel!

Psalm 128:6

Children's children are the crown of old men;
And the glory of children are their fathers.

Proverbs 17:6

T his is a book about grandparenting. If you picked it up expecting Dr. Ruth's tips for older lovers, I hope you saved your receipt! Several of my other books have advice for those who are no longer in their teens, twenties, or even thirty-something. This is a book about one of life's great transitions and the challenges it presents.

Why Am I Writing a Book about Grandparenting?

In many ways this is the book I have been waiting all my life to write. It is the product of a lifetime of personal experience and study and the culmination of a journey in which I have survived several wars, lived in three continents, experienced marriage, divorce, parenthood, and, most recently, been widowed.

My grandparents were a major part of my life during the first and happiest part of my own childhood. I spent every vacation until age ten on my maternal grandparents' farm in Wiesenfeld, Germany. Since I was their first grandchild, grandmother Pauline and grandfather Moses inevitably spoiled me a little. Even when I misbehaved (at age five or six I released all the geese from their pen into the village), my punishments were not overly harsh. I was doted upon not only by my grandparents, but also by my mother's five younger brothers and sisters. I always had a marvelous time in Wiesenfeld.

During the rest of the year, I lived in Frankfurt with my paternal grandmother and parents in a small four-room apartment. Here, as an only child, I had the spotlight to myself and received vast amounts of attention. Every Sunday my grandmother Selma would take me to the park where we would meet her sister and other friends who had brought their grandchildren. I think I inherited the talkativeness that has served me so well in my career from Grandma Selma. She was a wonderful presence in my life. Both my summers on the farm and my long talks with grandmother Selma taught me how important an extended family, and particularly grandparents, can be to a child.

All this was swept away with the rise of Hitler, World War II, and the Holocaust. In 1939, my parents and grandparents, in an act of unbelievable self-denial and sacrifice, sent me to safety in Switzerland. They all perished.

During the next twenty years, I grew up and studied early childhood education, psychology, and family systems. I lived in Switzerland, Israel, France, and the United States. I married, divorced, and remarried. Only with the birth of my first child, Miriam, in 1957, did I once again have a two-generation family. In 1961, I married my third husband, Fred Westheimer, and we remained happily married for more than thirty-six years until his recent death. In 1963, our son Joel was born.

For more than fifty years I lived in a one- or two-generation family. This changed in 1990 when my first grandchild, Ari, was born. Although I had eagerly anticipated becoming a grandmother, my first feeling on seeing Ari was a certain sadness. Sadness that my parents never had a chance to see their grandchildren, much less their beautiful great-grandchild. I realized later that in a real sense my parents and grandparents were getting new life through Ari. And I meant this not only in a symbolic sense. Their genes, their good qualities of health, intelligence, and compassion were literally in him. I was also struck by the thought that Hitler did not succeed, that the birth of Ari was one more proof of his defeat.

I *love* being a grandmother. From the time he was born I have spent a lot of time with Ari, and I have found that the best times are when we are alone together. From the outset I let Miriam and her husband Joel know that I was available to babysit, but only if Ari was going to be alert and awake for at least some of the time. If they just wanted someone to sit at home and watch TV or read a book while he slept, they could find someone else! When Ari was still a small baby, I went hiking with him and his parents in the Swiss Alps. I was more than happy to push his stroller. I walked very fast so that the others would not catch up with us and we could be alone. And I took him to Walt Disney World, just the two of us.

In 1996, Ari's sister Leora, my second grandchild, arrived. And as she's grown, I've enjoyed developing a special individual relationship with her as well. Leora is a terrific, spunky little girl. Her running toward me when I visit makes my heart jump. In January 1998, my son Joel and his wife, Barbara, had their first child, another granddaughter, Michal. What happiness! The grandparenting part of my life just gets richer and richer.

Beyond my personal experience, my interest in grandparents also stems from my long-running interest in the family. Long before I became "Dr. Ruth," I had studied and written about the family. My M.A. thesis was about German-Jewish children who, like myself, were sent to Switzerland at the time of the Holocaust.

So it was very much a return to my roots when in 1992 I served as executive producer for a PBS documentary, *Surviving Salvation*, which looked at the lives and families of Ethiopian refugees in Israel. Having lived as a refugee, having taught Yemenite children when they first arrived in Israel in the 1950s, and having experienced firsthand the manner in which migration can challenge family ties, I felt a special affinity for these people despite the vast cultural differences that separated us. At the same time as I worked on the movie, I coauthored (also with Steve Kaplan) *Surviving Salvation: The Ethiopian Jewish Family in Transition*. One of the most important points to emerge in that book was the dramatic way the position of grandparents and other elders had been undermined in the course of the group's wholesale immigration to Israel. Almost overnight, they went from being respected elders whose experience and wisdom were a valued resource for their entire community to being pensioners who were perceived by their children and grandchildren and immigration authorities as more of a burden than an asset. Unlike Moses, this "generation of the wilderness" not only saw but also entered the Promised Land. Yet few of them have truly made it their home.

In 1996, I collaborated with my friend and frequent co-author, Ben Yagoda, on a book called *The Value of Family: A Blueprint for the Twenty-first Century*. One of the most striking things we discovered in preparing that volume was the extent to which "family" in America had come to mean "nuclear family," *sans* grandparents, uncles, aunts, cousins, etc. To cite one example, *The Making of the Modern Family*, a book published in 1975, is dedicated to the authors' grandparents, but the text itself includes only a handful of references to grandparents, all of them in its discussion of traditional premodern families! Given all the subjects we had to cover in our book, Ben and I weren't able to devote nearly as much space as we wanted to grandparents. I knew that another book was needed.

If before the sexual revolution of the 1960s very few people were talking and writing about sex, the same can be said today about grandparenting. What makes this all the more remarkable is that we are on the verge of a grandparenting revolution. As life spans continue to grow and the baby boomers move into grandparenthood, the number of grandparents is set to explode. According to Dr. Arthur Kronhaber, the President of the Foundation for Grandparenting and one of America's foremost experts on grandparents, there were more than 60 million grandparents in the United States in 1990. By the year 2000, he writes, there will be over 90 million! *Almost one out of every three Americans will be a grandparent!*

With this fact in mind, I joined last year with Pierre Lehu, who has been my "minister of communications" for more than fifteen years, in writing *Dr. Ruth Talks About Grandparents*. In that book, we tried to present grandparents from the grandchild's point of view and offered "advice for kids on making the most of a special relationship." Although that book was a pleasure to write and a great success, it also, as the Israelis say, left a taste for more. I began working on a documentary film, *No Missing Link*, which explores the role that grandparents have played in the transmission of tradition in the former Soviet Union. In the summer of 1997, I traveled with a film crew to Moscow, St. Petersburg, and Uzbekistan in an attempt to document their story. Looking at Jews, Christians, and Muslims, that film examines the way in which grandparents kept the different religious heritages alive at a time when belief and practice were frowned upon by the communist regime.

At the same time, Steve Kaplan and I decided to renew our collaboration and write this book. There were a number of reasons why I chose Steve as my collaborator for this volume. First and foremost were the fun and success we had in our previous joint effort. However, there was an important additional reason. I wanted a coauthor who had insight into the experience and perspective of today's parents, the so-called "sandwich" generation, which is raising children *and* conducting an ongoing relationship with their own parents—their children's grandparents.

All too often books *for* grandparents are also books *by* grandparents and are presented solely from the grandparents' point of view. At their worst these books become a grandparents' version of the recent bestseller for single women, *The Rules*.

One author writes, "People also ask, 'How are you going to keep from giving advice?' I'm not. Grandparents are supposed to advise, even manipulate. The trick is to manipulate parents into making correct decisions without their realizing they've been manipulated. This is the Second Rule of Grandparenthood."

I think it's rather sad if as a grandparent your communication with your adult children is so bad and your estimation of their intelligence and decision-making abilities so low that you feel you have to manipulate them. If you've read any of my books, you know that I feel people shouldn't be manipulated. While I knew that this wasn't the sort of advice I'd give, I knew it would be only natural for me to look at things from the grandparents' perspective. Steve and most of his friends are parents, but not grandparents. He tends, naturally, to look at things from the middle generation's point of view. In writing this book, I found that it was crucial to have both generations' input if we were to achieve the balance we wanted.

The material in this book can be divided into three types: information, advice, and resources.

Information. One of the things I've learned from my own experience and from the numerous other books I've written is that it's impossible to make informed, intelligent decisions without accurate, reliable information. This is true for grandparenting as it is for choosing a birth control method or deciding which school to attend. One thing I've tried to do is to include in almost every chapter of this book a capsule description of what is known today about that particular aspect of grandparenting, whether it's gift-giving, adoption, travel, or discipline. In some chapters, particularly "Grandparents as Parents" and "Until Divorce Do Us Part", I've only been able to scratch the surface of very complex subjects that have vast psychological and legal ramifications. Despite the valiant efforts of a number of pioneering scholars (most of whose works are listed at the end of this book), there is still much we don't know about grandparenting. This book tries to provide as accurate a picture as possible of the current state of knowledge on grandparenting and the grandparents' place in the family.

Advice. Unfortunately, there are a lot of misconceptions about grandparents and a lot of ignorance about grandparenting. One of the most common misconceptions about grandparenting is that it comes naturally. Somehow, when your first grandchild is born, you suddenly know just what to do in every situation. For many years, this was the common perception of parenting. Parents, usually mothers, were assumed to know how to care for their children. At most, they learned by experience, their own and that of older and wiser women in the community. In 1946, the late Dr. Benjamin Spock became something of a trendsetter when he wrote what became a classic work, *The Common Sense Book of Baby and Child Care.* Its popularity is testified to by the over 40 million copies sold and the many books that have been written that seek to copy his success. There are so many books about parenting on the market today, it seems that we've gone to the opposite extreme in assuming that nothing about parenting comes naturally.

Grandparenting, in contrast, is comparatively neglected. When Ari was born, I was immediately struck by how many books were available to his parents, Miriam and Joel, and how few there were for me. The advice and information in this book will try, to some small degree, to remedy this situation. In it I will try to consider some of the most common issues facing grandparents and offer some guidance on how to achieve your goals as a grandparent.

From the outset, grandparents have one big advantage over parents. We're older and, hopefully, wiser. We bring to this new stage in our lives the lessons we've learned from countless other relationships.

Being a grandparent is, first and foremost, a relationship or a series of relationships with your grandchildren, children, spouse, and in-laws. It's not something you do on your own when you're alone, it's something that you share with those around you. There are many things that make it special, and other things that make it unique and different from any other relationship you have or have ever had. But it also has a lot in common with your other relationships. In grandparenting, as in any relationship, the keys to success are communication, honesty, supportiveness, generosity of spirit, openness, and patience. The rest, as the rabbis taught, is commentary. Since I've done very well over the past few years giving advice, I'll offer a fair amount of commentary in this book.

Resources. It's impossible in a single book to include all the available information there is about any subject, especially one so complex and varied as grandparenting. Many of the topics I consider, such as passing on family traditions, divorce, child custody, and gift giving, are the subjects of books all their own. Since I wanted to prepare a book and not a multivolume encyclopedia, I decided the only way to do justice to many of these topics was to offer guidance on where to find more information. I provide a selection of some of the most useful books for further reading on grandparenting in general and on specific topics covered in this book. I also offer a guide to the organizations and many nongovernmental bodies that provide support and advice on issues of concern to grandparents. I have found, too, that the Information Super Highway is chock full of information of interest and benefit to grandparents.

Although many of you may find this overwhelming, I felt I would be seriously remiss if I did not offer my readers some guidance on this resource. For those with even minimal computer literacy, the world is truly at your fingertips. Resources on specific topics are found at the end of each chapter, while the most important general sources are found at the end of the book.

I began this introduction by indicating that it is not a book of tips for older lovers. There are, at least, two other things you won't find in this book. Although I have tried to include a great deal of information about (grand)children, this is not a book about *parenting*. The best advice I can give to grandparents about parenting is that *you must always remember that you are not the parent*. Other than that, the best books for you to read on parenting are the ones your grandchild's parents are reading. It will give you valuable insight into their choices and childraising philosophy. The better you understand the background to their decisions and choices, the easier it will be for you to find your place in the new, expanded family system.

This is also not a book about aging. Although many of the best articles about grandparents and grandparenting appear in journals such as *Applied Gerontology* or *Aging and Human Development*, gerontology is a vast subject of which grandparenting is only one part. Moreover, as I discuss at several points in the book, grandparenting is increasingly a phenomenon of middle, not old, age. Many grandparents are not elderly. Indeed, the association between grandparenting and old age is one of the stereotypes we need to free ourselves from. At some points in the book, I will address some of the ways in which the aging process affects grandparenting. My goal here, however, is not to discuss aging in its entirety, but rather to look at a special relationship that involves not only those in their sixties and seventies, but also those in their fifties, forties, and, in some cases, even younger. Besides, becoming a grandparent is not something that happens to you automatically as you age. It's a special connection that no one generation can produce on its own.

Grandparenting is such a rich experience, and this book will only scratch the surface on many issues. Maybe this will become a whole new career for me? You can never tell. What I do know is that as we approach the dawn of a new millennium, there is every indication that the twenty-first century is going to mark a turning point in the history of grandparenting. Not only will there be more of us than ever before, but many of us will enjoy this special role for two, three, or even four decades.

The future is ours, so let's live it fully, starting today!

I

The Grandparent Relationship

Grandparents are our continuing tie to the near-past, to the events and beliefs and experiences that so strongly affect our lives and the world around us. Whether they are our own or surrogate grandparents who fill some of the gaps in our mobile society, our senior generation also provides our society a link to our national heritage and traditions.

We all know grandparents whose values transcend passing fads and pressures, and who possess the wisdom of distilled pain and joy. Because they are usually free to love and guide and befriend the young without having to take daily responsibility for them, they can often reach out past pride and fear of failure and close the space between generations.

President Jimmy Carter
September 9, 1979
Proclamation of National Grandparents' Day

Ready or Not . . .

Take a deep cleansing breath and don't push! That's probably one of the things your daughter or daughter-in-law is
being told in preparation for childbirth. It's not bad advice for
prospective grandparents as well!

Although there are lots of classes preparing new parents for
childbirth, similar frameworks for expectant grandparents are
(pardon the expression) in their infancy and are not available
in most communities. Whether you're bursting with excitement or simply shocked, you'd better start preparing yourself
for life's next great transition: grandparenthood.

If things seem totally out of control, that's probably because
they are. You probably decided when you wanted to marry and
begin raising a family, but there's really very little that you can
do regarding if and when you become a grandparent. It may
happen well before you expected or only after years of anticipation. Pressuring your children to marry and make you a
grandparent doesn't seem to have much effect. But if you're
reading this book, you probably have a grandchild or at least
one on the way.

Becoming a grandparent, like any other new stage in our
lives, produces a wide variety of reactions. You may be thrilled
or dismayed, surprised or relieved. Whatever your initial
response to impending grandparenthood, you'd better prepare yourself for the experience of a lifetime!

But I'm Not Ready!

I was already sixty-two when I became a grandmother for
the first time, and I was thrilled with my new status. I'm sure it
was one of the factors that eventually led me to stop dyeing my

hair. I don't mind looking like a grandmother. However, I know that not everyone is quite so excited at the prospect of becoming a grandparent.

"I'm too young to be a grandparent!" I hear you cry.

One of my favorite episodes in the popular 1980s family program "The Cosby Show" concerns the birth of their first grandchild. Mrs. Huxtable (actress Phylicia Rashad), an attractive and successful lawyer, was thrilled and deeply moved that her daughter had become a mother. But she clearly balked at being identified as a grandmother. Her dismay at being called "Grandma" was joked about on several shows. Both she and her in-laws agreed that they were too young to be grandparents. At the time these episodes were filmed, Ms. Rashad had just turned 40, not an unheard-of age for a grandparent but probably somewhat younger than the character she played, a professional woman whose daughter had already graduated college. Her distress at being labeled a grandmother ("I look so much younger than my grandmother did!") is a feeling shared by many other women.

For reasons I think we all can understand, women often have a harder time than men with the image of grandparents as old people. However, this isn't always the case. Take Steve Martin's character in the recent film *Father of the Bride II*. He dyes his hair, starts frantically exercising, and generally turns his life upside down when he discovers that he's going to be a grandfather. Impending grandfatherhood can trigger a male crisis and make many a man feel as if his better days are behind him.

If the fact that you're about to become a grandparent pushes you to get into shape, I'm all for that. A physician-approved regimen of moderate exercise is highly recommended. Grandparenting is not for couch potatoes, and recent studies indicate that regular exercise has its benefits for all ages. But don't think that you're going to somehow turn back the clock, or that being in shape means that you're not really a grandparent. Contrary to some popular images, most grandparents are neither feeble nor old. Fifty percent of middle-aged adults (ages forty-five to fifty-nine) are grandparents.

Since people become grandparents at such different times in their lives (there's more variety here than there is for age of first marriage or age of first child), you may find yourself sharing an experience with people you've usually thought of as being of a different generation. Don't let that put you off. My experience is that whatever their age, grandparents have an instinctive link with each other.

In the final analysis, the only correct answer to the question "When is the right time to become a grandparent?" is when one of your children has a child. For better or worse, there's very little you can do about becoming a grandparent, regardless of your age.

Whatever problems you may have about becoming a grandparent too early, you must always remember that they are your problems and not your daughter and son-in-law's. (I will discuss the special case of teen pregnancies and unwed mothers in Chapter 10.) You should never let your concerns about age subtract from their happiness and excitement. Talk to friends who may have experienced something similar. Talk to a counselor, therapist, or member of the clergy. Don't make your children feel guilty that they're making you a grandparent.

*Remember, You Are a Grand*parent

grand: *adj.* magnificent or splendid; noble or fine; of great importance and distinction

In all the excitement over having a new grandchild, don't forget that you are still a parent. Every father has probably at one time or another told his daughter, "No matter how old you are, you'll always be my little girl." It's very easy to let your enthusiasm over your grandchildren distract your attention from your adult children. We often fail to remember our parenting roles and get caught up in the new experience.

Sometimes this happens even before the new grandchild arrives. One friend of mine was well into her ninth month of pregnancy when her birthday came along. All day long she received calls from family members asking how she was feeling and checking to be sure she hadn't gone to the hospital yet. No one wished her a happy birthday! She was devastated. "The baby's not even here and she's already getting all the attention," she cried.

Another friend said jokingly, "I can remember when my parents used to say hello to *me* and ask *me* questions when I came for a visit. Since they have grandchildren, it's almost as if I'm invisible when we arrive."

Although it's often overlooked, the birth of a grandchild offers lots of opportunities for you to be a grand**parent.** If it's their first child, your son or daughter will probably be both excited and scared. Everyone will be paying lots of attention to the new grandchild. Be special by paying attention to the parents. Find out in advance how you can be most helpful in the days immediately after the birth. Listen to them tell the story of the birth over and over. Buy a present for the proud mother and father, not just for the grandchild.

If it's a second or third child, there's probably lots you can do for the parents and your other grandchildren. You might offer to do some extra babysitting to give them some free time before the new baby arrives. As much as the parents will try to reassure their other children that they've gained a brother or sister, not lost their parents, it may be hard for them to believe that when everyone is paying so much attention to the new baby. How wonderful for your older grandchild that grandma bought her a favorite comic and came up to her room to read it with her, or that grandpa baked her favorite cookies and is having cookies and milk in the kitchen with her.

Remember that being a grandparent is a marathon, not a sprint. Long after the other well-wishers have come and gone, you will still be around. So when everyone else is fluttering around, cooing and aahing over the new baby, don't be just one more person making demands on the parents. Be the person they can count on.

Choosing a Name (for Yourself, Not for the Baby)

Your family may have particular traditions about the naming of children. Perhaps you would like your grandchild to be named after one of your parents or another beloved relative. If your son is John Jr., you may be hoping your grandson will be John III. If you are asked you should certainly express your preference, but even if your children do consult you, it's up to them to choose a name for the baby. You, on the other hand, get to decide what your grandchildren should call you.

While your children are browsing through the countless

books of baby names currently on the market, you can be thinking about whether you want to be called Grandmother, Grandma, Grans, Granny, Nana, or Nanny. Those are just some of the English choices. Maybe you want your grandchildren to use a term that reflects your ethnic background. In Greek, grandpa is *Papou*; in Italian, it's *Nonno*; in Swahili, it's *Babu*; and in Spanish, it's *Abuelo*.

Carolyn J. Booth and Mindy B. Henderson have recently published a delightful little book entitled *Grandmother by Another Name: Endearing Stories about What We Call Our Grandmothers*, in which they've collected stories of how grandmothers got their special names.

My grandchildren call me Omi. I asked my daughter, Miriam, to have them call me that because that's what I called my grandmother when I was a child living in Germany. Omi isn't the formal word for grandmother in German—that's *Grossmutter*—but it's an affectionate name that many children use. The grandchildren called my husband, Fred, Opa, although the real German term is *Grossvater*.

When Steve was growing up he called his mother's mother Grandma and his father's parents by the Yiddish terms Bubbe and Zayde. His children call his mother Grandma, and for their mother's parents they use the Hebrew, Savta and Saba.

Take advantage of the period before the birth to choose your new name—and wear it well and long.

Great Expectations

Learning to Listen

One of the most special times in any family's life are the months leading up to the birth of a child or grandchild. For the expectant grandparents, especially if this is your daughter or daughter-in-law's first child, this is a crucial time for building memories and sharing dreams. Whether you're around the corner or miles away, the months leading up to childbirth offer an excellent opportunity to learn about your children's hopes, fears, plans, and expectations. It's also a good time to begin practicing many of the skills that make for good grandparenting, such as holding your tongue, listening, and being supportive. As any successful grandparent has learned, there's a very good reason why we were created with two ears and one mouth: so we can listen (at least) twice as much as we talk.

One of the most important things you can do between the time you hear that you're going to be a grandparent and the birth of your grandchild is devote yourself to your relationship with your children. Open up the lines of communication. Find out what books they're reading about baby care and what decorating ideas they have. This is a wonderful time to begin discussing such topics as visits, babysitting, holiday celebrations, and gifts. You may want to go shopping with the expectant parents for clothes or baby furniture or raise the matter of a baby shower.

Although the birth of a grandchild can be a great unifier and bring together families that have been divided, don't count on that being enough. Most research indicates that the frequency of grandparents' contacts with their grandchildren are intimately connected to their relationship with their adult children, especially their daughters. According to Cherlin and Furstenberg's study *The New American Grandparent*, "grandparents who reported that their relationship with the study child's mother was 'extremely close' saw their grandchildren about twice as often as those who said 'fairly close' or 'not very close' . . . *Grandparents who want frequent contact with their grand-children need to get along well with their daughters or daughters-in-law. . . .*" (emphasis added)

I'm not suggesting that you should work on your relationship with your adult children in order to get more time with your grandchildren. You should do it because they're your children.

Almost inevitably, the grandfathers-to-be will have to make more of an effort than their wives will to be in on things. Mothers and daughters have the shared experience of pregnancy as a natural conversation piece. Grandfathers do share the father-in-waiting experience with their sons and sons-in-law, and it's important to use that as a basis to strengthen those ties. Don't forget that the father-to-be also has concerns and worries.

With a little bit of effort, almost every grandfather can find a way to share in the excitement and express his involvement. Whether it's painting the nursery with the mother-to-be or just sending along newspaper clippings of interest to an expectant couple, there are lots of things you can do to let them know you want to be part of the process.

Although it's natural that you devote most of your attention to your son or daughter, it's important to use the time before the birth to build your relationship with your in-laws as well. The birth of your grandchild means that you are now related by more than marriage. You will be sharing the joys and trials of your grandchildren for many years to come. Good communication will avoid future misunderstandings about gifts, holiday visits, vacation plans, and countless other areas in which your concerns overlap.

Learning to Talk the Talk

One way to ease your communication with your children during the pregnancy is to familiarize yourself with all the basic medical terms they'll be using. Whether it's an ultrasound exam or amniocentesis (one of several possible ways to detect genetic conditions), it will be easier to be involved if you know what medical procedures they're doing, what each one is called, and what information it provides. Although such tests are performed routinely to ensure that the fetus is developing normally, several of them also indicate whether it is a boy or a girl. Your children may have indicated that they don't want to know in advance; or they may be keeping the secret to themselves. Whatever their choice, respect their wishes and hold your peace.

Once you begin talking about the medical aspects of pregnancy, you may find it hard to stop. Although it's fine to share information and experiences, remember to be reassuring and supportive. The last thing an expectant couple needs to hear are stories about difficult deliveries or other mishaps. And always remember, not only aren't you the mother or father this time, you also aren't the doctor. Leave the medical advice to the professional they've chosen.

Health Matters

Even before you get involved in the knotty issues of child care and discipline, you're bound to have lots of questions about prenatal care and childbirth. It probably has been at least twenty years since you gave birth and, although the process of conception and birth are pretty much what they've been since time immemorial, many of the practices surrounding the birth have changed over that time.

Jokes about pickles and ice cream notwithstanding, expectant mothers often have very specific dietary needs. In recent years, these have followed the dietary trends among the general population, with an emphasis on fruits, vegetables, and low-fat milk products. Many doctors advise expectant mothers to avoid alcohol and caffeine. Smoking is strongly discouraged, of course. Although it's up to the expectant parents to adhere to the diet their doctor recommends, it's a good idea for you to inquire in advance before they come to visit you to be sure you have plenty of whatever they need.

Diet is only one of the recent trends in prenatal health care. One grandfather I know had always known that his smoking bothered his children. In recent years, his children had become increasingly critical of his habit. When his daughter-in-law became pregnant, she declared her house a no-smoking zone and made it clear that she didn't want him ever to smoke in his grandchild's presence. Needless to say, he was far from pleased, but he resigned himself to this new regimen.

The general proexercise spirit of our times has also had its impact on childbirth preparation. Gone are the days of lots of bed rest and strictly limited activity. Unless her doctor has specifically cautioned against it, the expectant mom is likely to be enrolled in an exercise class and may continue most of her normal activities, including travel, well into her pregnancy. One friend of mine continued to lead hiking groups well into her eighth month, and another went into labor during her aerobics class!

Birth Options
The past quarter-century has seen the growth of tremendous openness and diversity in the way couples handle the

childbirth experience. Only a generation ago, the father's involvement was limited to phoning the doctor, driving to the hospital, and pacing in the waiting room. Today, coaching and being present at the birth are commonplace. As the generation of those who pioneered natural childbirth move into grandparenthood, many are eager to share the same immediacy of experience at the birth of their grandchildren as well. Don't be embarrassed to raise this option with your children.

Whether you're present or not, be supportive of your children's choices for their child's birth. Whether it's natural childbirth or high-tech intervention, soothing music or hard rock, a birthing chair or a conventional hospital bed, it's their decision. If their physician approves, hold your tongue, whatever you may think of their ideas and preferences. It'll be good training for the many times you'll have to choose silence over conflict after your grandchild is born.

The New Arrival and Timing Your Arrival

One question that always comes up around the birth of a grandchild, particularly if the grandparents live far way, is when and for how long they should come to visit. Obviously, your first inclination will be to see your new grandchild as soon as possible, but it's a good idea to discuss this with the parents *before* the birth.

There was a time when new mothers spent as much as a week in the hospital recovering from the birth. These days, if there are no complications, forty-eight or even twenty-four hours is more common. Under such revolving-door policies, a visit to the hospital can barely be squeezed in and is often impossible if you live far away.

Once they've brought their new baby home, the new parents may prefer to spend the first few days bonding with their new baby. Your daughter-in-law may feel more comfortable if *her* mother comes to stay for the first few days, and dealing with two grandmothers (and two grandfathers) and the experience of a new baby all at once may be too much for her. On the other hand, she may welcome the presence of someone who can help with the laundry, cooking, or keeping a watchful eye on her other children. Discussing such issues in advance not only will help prevent misunderstandings at the last minute, it will also enable you to plan your schedule, arrange for vacation time, and do whatever else is necessary for a successful visit. Even if you decide to delay your first visit for a while, you can send flowers or other gifts.

Steve's mother, for example, waited almost three months before visiting her grandson overseas. She knew that the other grandparents were close by and ready to offer any immediate assistance needed. "At three months, the baby will be more alert and the parents will be more relaxed," she explained.

Welcoming the New Family Member

One of the touchiest issues for many families is how to commemorate the birth of a child. Many young couples give little thought to the place of religion in their family until the first child arrives, so discreet inquiries about their plans for a baptism, christening, brit (bris), or other ceremony may push them to begin thinking about their plans. For couples who come from different religious or cultural traditions, the celebration of their first child's birth often serves to highlight the differences in their traditions or between their ritual preferences and those of either or both sets of grandparents. Disagreements over such issues are among the hardest to resolve amicably.

Unfortunately, there are no magic formulas in this case, or in the many other instances of differing rituals and traditions, some of which I discuss in the next chapter. It's best to sound out your children on their plans before the birth. This will avoid unpleasant surprises caused by mistaken assumptions and will give everyone a chance to think a little before the birth itself. If you're lucky, you may have some special family traditions that you can pass on with the blessing of all involved, even if you can't do everything you'd hoped.

Don't Forget to Celebrate Yourself!

In all the excitement about the new baby and the concern you have for your children, it's easy to forget one very important person: YOU.

Dr. Lillian Carson, author of *The Essential Grandparent: A Guide to Making a Difference*, suggests that grandparents should create their own rituals to mark their transition into a new stage of the life cycle. Perhaps you wish to sponsor a *kiddush* at your local synagogue in honor of your new status, go to church, or just have a quiet dinner with some friends. As Dr. Carson says, "Your rite can be anything you want it to be." What's important is that it be a meaningful way for you to mark your entry into grandparenthood.

Although it's been almost twenty years since President Jimmy Carter proclaimed National Grandparents' Day, it really hasn't caught on as an annual holiday. Its content, like so much about grandparenting, remains vague and undefined. Even if florists and the general public haven't made it the same sort of big event as Valentine's Day or Mother's Day, there's no reason not to celebrate it! The next time your children call you on Father's Day or your anniversary, remind them that Grandparents' Day is the second Sunday in September. Until they catch on, celebrate it yourself with a special treat or by being in touch with your grandchildren. Perhaps a group of your friends who are also grandparents would like to celebrate the day together.

Anthropologists and psychologists have taught us that rites of passage serve a vital function in the lives of individuals and societies. On the personal level, they assist us in our transition from one stage in life to another. Rites of passage remind us of our place in the circle of life and help us to announce and share with others our entry into a new role. On a larger social level, they enable us to identify with our traditions and the generations that preceded us and blazed a path for us.

Whether you want to let the whole world know or share the news more intimately with your nearest and dearest, don't pass over *your* transition in silence.

I wanted to shout it to the world: *I'm a Grandparent!!!!*

Common Concerns

Although every family is different and every grandparent has different issues, there are certain themes and questions that recur frequently. This chapter explores these common concerns, common because they appear in many families and because you share them with your grandchild's parents.

As I said in my introduction, this is not a book about parenting. Bookstores are already full of volumes on that subject, and it's not my intention to add another. But grandparenting doesn't take place in a vacuum. Perhaps the most important key to being an effective grandparent is sensitivity to the needs of our children and their children. The more we understand what it's like to be a parent and a child at the dawn of a new millennium, the better grandparenting we'll do.

A Balancing Act

Today's parents face many challenges that were unthinkable only a few generations ago. None of these is greater than the need to balance the demands of work with those of family. As recently as 1960, only 38 percent of women were in the paid labor force. Among married women with children under age six, this figure was even lower, at 19 percent. All this began to change rather dramatically in the early 1970s as more and more mothers sought paid employment. In fact, many of today's younger grandparents were the trendsetters when they were parents. By 1996, the number of working married women with small children had more than tripled, to 64 percent. Among single mothers, the numbers are even higher. According to some estimates, by the year 2000, 80 percent of all mothers with children under the age of six will be in the labor force.

The conventional wisdom is that this development was a direct result of the women's liberation movement. Although there is some truth to this view, the reality is a great deal more complicated. This trend actually *preceded* the women's movement. There were strong economic reasons for this development. One obvious way for a family to maintain a relatively high standard of living in the face of developing economic insecurity and a decline in real wages is to have two incomes. Many, if not most, of these women entering the workforce had discovered an uncomfortable truth. Born in an age of economic abundance and raised to expect a continually improving standard of living, they entered the job market only to find that well-paying jobs were hard to come by. As real purchasing power declined, the mothers of young children began taking jobs en masse.

As women have entered the workforce in growing numbers, their household responsibilities have declined only in part. Single mothers, of course, are required both to support their children and to maintain their households. But even after years of prodding, the number of husbands who share equally in household duties is still comparatively small. According to recently published figures, married women continue to be responsible for two-thirds of all work done in the house, devoting 35.1 hours a week to household chores versus 17.4 hours by their husbands.

One immediate result of this increased work time is a decrease in the time parents spend with children. According to one study, the average parent has fifty hours less free time per month than a decade ago. A story in the *New York Times* in 1995 noted that the average child spends three hours a day with a parent, 40 percent less than in 1960. Although any number of advice columns and books have tried to convince today's parents that it's the *quality* not the *quantity* of time that matters in parenting, most remain unconvinced. A 1991 Gallup Poll showed that one-half of employed mothers and two-thirds of fathers thought they were spending too little time with their children.

There are several indications that as a nation we have failed to adjust to the reality of the past quarter-century and have failed dismally to provide high-quality child-care programs. In the 1990 National Child Care Survey, 26 percent of parents indicated that they would prefer some other kind of child-care arrangements. The unease that many parents feel regarding the care for their children is expressed vividly in films such as *The Hand That Rocks the Cradle* and in the public's fascination with the recent trial of the British nanny, Louise Woodward. It also has a clear basis in reality. According to the Children's Defense Fund, in 1996 only one in seven child-care centers and one in ten family child-care homes are of a high enough quality to enhance children's development.

Is it any wonder that many families, particularly mothers, have sought out ingenious solutions such as job sharing, telecommuting, and home businesses—all in an attempt to achieve a balance between economic necessity and family needs? A growing number have also reversed the dominant trend and have been able to stop working altogether. A Virginia organization, Mothers at Home, was created to help mothers "at home realize they made a great choice" and "excel at a job for which no one feels fully prepared"; it has more than 15,000 members nationwide.

I applaud these women for taking what in many social circles amounts to a courageous step; a woman who does *not* work is sometimes stupidly seen as less intelligent than one who does. But at the same time, in no way do I denigrate those who are still in the workplace, women who are forced to suffer their own pangs of guilt about not living up to the ideal.

Although the percentage of fathers who are primary caregivers for preschoolers seems to be more a factor of economics than choice (it shot up from 15 percent in 1988 to 20 percent in 1991 but returned to 15 percent in 1993), still, over a million fathers have chosen this option.

As a grandparent, your goal is to respect and support your children's choices so there will be no needless guilt. Whatever the child-care arrangement you decided upon when you were raising your kids, you must always keep in mind that your choice for *your* children doesn't have to be your children's choice for your grandchildren. If you went out to work and made arrangements for daycare, you have to learn to respect your daughter/daughter-in-law's (or son/son-in-law's) decision to stay at home. At the same time, even if you decided to stay home and put your career on hold, you can't expect your children to make the same choice.

When I was working with Ben Yagoda on our book *The Value of Family*, I clipped a letter to the *New York Times* from a Maryland woman that made this point very well, though it was concerned with different parenting styles and not grandparent-parent relations:

> Two groups of mothers are on the defensive today: full-time mothers who worry about their lapsed careers and full-time employees who worry about their children. Discourse between them has become virtually impossible. Mothers in each group have a troubling tendency to justify their child-care decisions by making sweeping attacks on the other group. . . .
>
> Years ago a study found that the best predictor of success for children was happy parents: whether their mothers worked or stayed home proved immaterial. . . .
>
> I hope that women will someday have enough self-confidence to justify their own decisions without denigrating the choices that are made by others, and to read the conclusions of noted child-care experts with more detachment.

Who's the Boss?

She thinks the young women of the present too forward, and the men not respectful enough; but hopes her grandchildren will be better; though she differs with her daughter in several points respecting their management.

Leigh Hunt (1784–1859), *The Old Lady*

The stay-at-home versus working mother controversy is just one of the many topics on which your experience and your children's plans may be in conflict. Other common areas of conflict include education (public/private/parochial), food, clothing, and manners. It seems that there are always at least two opinions about every aspect of child care. If you're the type of person who believes that the two opinions are *yours* and the *wrong* one, you're not going to be a very popular grandparent.

What are you to do when you disagree with the way your children are raising your grandchild? In many ways, this is the simplest question to answer and the hardest advice to carry out. Put briefly and succinctly, unless they are doing something that is immoral, illegal, or obviously dangerous, keep your mouth shut. And when I say keep your mouth shut, that means avoiding obvious criticisms as well as leading questions like "Oh, is that how *you* give her a bath?" or "Do most of your friends' kids watch so much television?"

Remember, you had your chance to raise your kids your way. Now it's their turn.

As the earlier Leigh Hunt quotation indicates, grandparents have probably been second-guessing their children as long as there have been grandparents. One indication of the frequency with which this problem comes up is its constant recurrence in recent television shows. If in the 1950s grandparents were almost invisible on American family television, in the 1980s and 1990s their presence has all too often been portrayed as the bane of their children's existence. Nothing seems to disrupt the parents' lives as much as a visit from grandma and grandpa. This may not be a case of art imitating life, but there certainly is a kernel of truth.

The other day, I was watching a rerun of the popular television show "Step by Step," which stars Suzanne Somers and

Patrick Duffy as Carol and Frank Lambert, parents of a blended family: three of his children, three of her children, and one born to both of them. What caught my attention was that Frank's mother was coming to visit her newest grandchild. From the minute she walked in the door, poor Carol was under attack. According to her mother-in-law, she didn't know how to choose a fabric softener, coax a burp, or start the baby on solid food. *Nana's gonna teach mommy how to do all the right things* was the newly arrived grandmother's message, not only to her new granddaughter but to the rest of the grand- and step-grandchildren. *"Nana's in charge this week!,"* she proudly proclaimed as she encouraged two of the teenage boys to have ice cream cones before supper. Finally, Frank stood up to his mother and reminded her that this was Carol's house. "There's only room for one Mrs. Lambert in this house, and it's Carol," he told his mother. But what really drove the message home was his mother's realization that she was acting just like her mother-in-law had when she was a young mother! *"I've become my own mother-in-law! Carol must hate me!"*

In this episode, Carol Lambert was an experienced mother with three children of her own and three stepchildren. Even so, her mother-in-law's criticisms hurt her, undermined her authority, and interfered with her relationship with her husband. Just imagine the impact if she had been a young mother raising her first child or living in her in-laws' house.

Undermining your children's self-confidence is a no-win situation. It hurts their relationship to their children, and it usually hurts their relationship with you. In particular, you must remember that in dealing with disagreements about your grandchildren, *never criticize your children in front of their children!* To do so is always a mistake. Your children will almost certainly be hurt, and their defensiveness will probably prevent them from heeding your advice anyway. Your grandchildren, sensing the discomfort of the people they love and admire most in the world, will also feel bad and blame you.

If you must discuss a particular situation with your children, do so in private. Remember, you are the grandparent, not the parent. Just as you're going to have your own style of grandparenting that suits you, your children will have their own style of parenting. You are not there to coach (unless asked), but to be a cheerleader.

I know that you will find it almost impossible to follow this advice completely, but the harder you try, the better it will be for everyone. The better you understand the way your grandchildren are being raised and the issues that are of most importance to your children, the better off you will be. Perhaps it's the foods that they eat or the toys that they play with. It may be the way they are disciplined or the television shows that they watch. It's important to remember that there are fads and fashions in child care as in everything else.

Spare the Rod and Spoil the Grandchild?

One of the many wonderful things about being "Dr. Ruth" is that so many people have heard my name and take an interest in what I do. For example, the minute I started telling people that I was working on a book about grandparenting, they started sending me clippings, articles, and, in some cases, even books about grandparenting.

In one of the newspaper articles I received, a psychologist and new grandparent had the following advice to his adult children: "It's your job to never spoil this child. It's our job as grandparents to always spoil him. We will have no problems as long as we don't try to do one another's jobs."

Although I know he meant this advice somewhat tongue-in-cheek, I had to cringe. I suppose because his grandson was only six months old at the time, the writer had very little experience with what he was writing about. If he had, he might have realized that this was a recipe for trouble. All he'd have to do is talk to a friend of mine, whose parents not only bring their grandchildren vast amounts of candy, but *wake them up at night to offer it to them*!

Rules and discipline are clearly the responsibility of the child's parents, but when you're with your grandchildren, although you may not have to enforce the discipline, you do have to follow the rules. One of the sure ways to strain your relationship with your children is to create situations in which they're always having to play bad cop to your good cop.

Say that you're visiting your daughter and granddaughter and it's half an hour before supper. Your granddaughter asks you if she can have a snack. If you know that she's not allowed to snack before supper, you have to tell her no. If you don't know the rules, you have to tell her to ask her mother. Giving her a snack will only encourage her to come to you whenever she wants to get around her parents. It's a bad lesson for her, and it will hurt your relationship with your children as well. Just as parents have to be consistent and back each other up in dealing with their children, grandparents also have to be sensitive to these issues.

A friend of mine thought she had found a good compromise on this one. She told her granddaughter, "It's all right with me if you have a snack, but ask your mother." Although she thought she was being helpful by giving her daughter the final word, her daughter didn't appreciate being repeatedly cast in the role of the villain. After all, the same grandmother probably wouldn't have said, "I don't think you should, but ask your mother." What's the fun in that?

Although it's commonly assumed that parents are in charge of discipline and grandparents are there to spoil, this is not always the case. In fact, one of the most common complaints today's grandparents have about today's parents is that they don't exert enough authority over their children. "They just let the kids run wild!" they complain. In part, this probably reflects the fact that it's hard to be the one spoiling the children if the parents don't draw the line somewhere. It also seems to reflect the less authoritarian form of parenting that is currently in vogue.

One friend told me the following story: "At the end of every one of my parent's visits, my father and I have a private talk. This time, he wanted to talk about the grandchildren and discipline. 'The kids are great,' he said, 'but you really need to exert more authority. Everything would be much easier if instead of discussing everything with them, you just told them what you had decided.'"

"I told him it was a good idea," my friend said, "and I'd talk it over with the kids!"

My friend's father was not alone. One recent study showed that one of the biggest criticisms grandparents have about their children's parenting is that they didn't exercise enough discipline with the grandchildren. Their feelings were somewhat mixed, however, because the thing they admired most about the parent-grandchild relationship was the closeness and informality! There may be a connection between the two, but go figure. . . .

Whether your children are stricter than you'd like or too easygoing for your taste, you need to figure out how you can be part of the wider picture. As a grandparent, you don't make up the rules of the game, but you still have to play by them. And of course, one of the great things about being a grandparent is that you don't have to play when you're tired, or annoyed, or when you've just had enough. I'm not suggesting that you get in the habit of picking up your toys and going home in a huff. But remember, unlike a parent, you are *not* the one responsible for discipline or most of the other essentials of raising your grandchildren.

One major exception to these rules occurs when you are left in charge of the grandchildren, whether for an hour or for a few days. For most children, having their parents away is disruptive enough in and of itself. For the very young, even an afternoon can seem like forever, and for the older ones, a long weekend can seem very, very long. In general, this is not a good time to try to introduce all sorts of changes in their routine. However, one change is essential. Before the parents leave, be sure they make it 100 percent clear to their children that in their absence *you are in charge!*

Traditions: Preserving, Adapting, and Inventing Them

Nothing seems to give families a sense of continuity and their members a sense of belonging so much as the special customs and practices that are passed down year after year, generation after generation. Whether it's the annual Labor Day picnic with all the cousins, aunts, and uncles or Mother's Day dinner prepared by the children, having a unique way of observing certain occasions is part of what gives each of us a feeling of our family's uniqueness and cohesiveness. One family I know has always spent New Year's Eve in church, viewing it as a time for reflection and prayer, rather than celebration and parties. (Although the children protested as they got older, their mother's iron will usually prevailed.) Another family regularly sits down to a Christmas dinner at which the main dish is oyster stew. As strange as some of these traditions may appear to outsiders, to members of the family they somehow seem natural—a mark of distinctiveness and of a special connection to each other.

One of the pleasures of moving into the more senior ranks in the family hierarchy is that you increasingly become an authority on the history of and the proper way of observing your family's particular customs. However, the minute your children begin to marry and raise families of their own, the concept of family traditions becomes infinitely more complex. At the least, the new family (husband and wife) will have inherited two sets of family traditions, and at times these will be at odds with each other. They can't have Christmas dinner with both sets of in-laws at the same time, and even if they're at your house for the holiday, your in-laws' special traditions may be different from yours. The centerpiece of one family's Fourth of July may be a barbecue, whereas another family has always watched the fireworks while having a late dinner at a hilltop restaurant.

So long as there are no grandchildren involved, a young couple may have been prepared to go along with the way things are, by alternating holidays or even splitting the day. As their family grows, however, there will probably be more and more occasions on which they want to do it their way. This is a natural part of the progression by which they form their own family with its own traditions.

Holidays are only one of the many areas in which family traditions prevail. For example, it may be that boys in your family have attended the same private school for four generations. Even if it's your deepest wish that your grandson continue this family tradition, you have little choice but to defer to his parents if they make another choice.

One way to avoid at least some of the conflicts that can arise is to focus on traditions that emphasize your relationship with your children and grandchildren as individuals and that don't require everyone's participation or assent to work. For example, in one family I know, the grandparents take a grandchild out to dinner at the restaurant of his choice to mark his graduation from high school, college, or graduate school. In another, the grandparents have a ten-to-one charity policy. For every dollar their granddaughter donates to a particular charity, they give ten. The money involved is secondary to the discussions they share on the choice of charity and the lessons they share on the importance of giving to the less fortunate.

It's usually helpful if you keep two things in mind about traditions. First, traditions are meaningful because they have meaning, not because they're traditions. If you're a member of the British royal family, you may feel that you have to continue a certain tradition, even if no one enjoys it, because it's expected (and even that seems to be changing!). But if you're just ordinary folk, you should never lose sight of the fact that traditions are about our links to the past and our ties to the present. Pressuring children and grandchildren to observe a tradition because you've always done it that way is usually counterproductive. That doesn't mean you can't give them a gentle nudge, but be prepared to concede graciously.

Second, remember that traditions are constantly being invented and reinvented. If you think back carefully, you can probably remember several instances in which you developed new family traditions as your children grew up. Some of these will continue to be practiced by your children and grandchildren. Some of these may skip a generation as your grandchildren, enthralled by your stories, may decide to revive a custom passed over by their parents. Just because you're a grandparent doesn't mean your creative days are over. New traditions of grandparenting are being invented every day.

If at First You Don't Succeed . . .

Although it may be your goal to be the perfect grandparent, that's not any more realistic than trying to be a perfect parent. You'll be putting tons of pressure on yourself and probably on everyone around you. It's probably much more realistic to try to be a "good enough" grandparent and learn from you mistakes as you go along.

As any other relationship, grandparenting has to be worked on. It's no more natural than being a parent, and we all know how much learning *that* involves. In recognition of this fact, over the past decade, Robert and Shirley Strom of Arizona State University have pioneered the idea of grandparent education. Working through churches, senior centers, and community colleges, they have made a major contribution to strengthening the grandparenting role and through it building stronger families. Their courses, which meet in twelve weekly sessions, seek (1) to acquaint grandparents with the goals parents have today, (2) to discover what it's like to be growing up now, and (3) to recognize how family changes call for shifts in the roles of grandparents. Both grandparents and parents have generally found that such formal learning by the older generations improves communication and mutual understanding. The course materials, as well as a guide to establishing a grandparent education program, have been published and are listed in the Further Reading section of this chapter.

You may not be inclined toward or have available a formal course in grandparent education. This doesn't mean that you shouldn't relate to grandparenting as a learning experience. One of the keys to being the grandparent you want to be is to learn from experience. Every moment you spend with your grandchild you're receiving vast amounts of feedback.

One friend of mine does this by keeping diaries. She originally thought of the idea as a living history of her grandchildren, an ongoing story. Very quickly she realized that her entries resembled in many ways the records she had kept of her classes when she'd been a junior high teacher. Looking back at what she had written she had a record of her successes and failures as a grandparent. What games had worked or not? Which books or toys were appropriate for which ages? What foods did they like? How long until the youngest grandchild got tired or bored? By building on experience, much as she had as a teacher, she was able to learn from the rough times as much or even more than from the fun times, to everyone's benefit.

I'm not suggesting that it's necessary to document every aspect of your experience so formally, but a little bit of evaluation can go a long way. Among the things to keep track of are good times for visits, types of help that the parents really welcome, plus food and music preferences. How many times have you heard a complaint about a relationship that starts out, "Every time we get together . . ."? If you don't learn from your experiences, both good and bad, that's what is likely to happen. If you begin each get-together with a little more information, your chances of achieving your goals are vastly improved.

Further Reading

ADAMS, JANE. *I'm Still Your Mother: How to Get Along with your Grown-up Children for the Rest of Your Life* (New York: Delta, 1995), Chapter 8.

STROM, ROBERT and SHIRLEY. *Becoming a Better Grandparent: A Guidebook for Strengthening the Family* (Newbury Park, CA: Sage, 1991).

————. *Becoming a Better Grandparent: Viewpoints of Strengthening the Family* (Newbury Park, CA.: Sage, 1991).

————. *Grandparent Education: A Guide for Leaders* (Newbury Park, CA: Sage, 1991).

————. *Achieving Grandparent Potential: A Guidebook for Building Intergenerational Relationships* (Newbury Park, CA: Sage, 1992).

————. *Achieving Grandparent Potential: Viewpoints on Building Intergenerational Relationships* (Newbury Park, CA: Sage, 1992).

3

Grandparenting:
A Developing Relationship

Whether it's a toddler going through the terrible twos or a teen who has just had his nose pierced, we've all said or been told that a child or grandchild was "just going through a phase." This little bit of reassurance has a firm basis in psychological fact. People—children as well as adults—do go through phases or stages as they develop physically and emotionally.

One of the keys to being a successful grandparent is finding ways to be helpful and supportive that are appropriate for your grandchildren's ages, their parent's needs, and the particular stages in their lives. It may sound simple, but when you try to describe this on paper it can seem enormously complicated. Not only may you have several grandchildren in a single family at different stages of their lives, but their parents' situation will also be evolving. A struggling young couple may need one kind of support when their first child is a toddler, but their situation may be completely different a decade later when their third or fourth child reaches that age. In addition, you'll be a decade older and you may have more time but less money, or less stamina but more experience.

In order to keep things simple and clear, this chapter is organized around the stages that one grandchild would go through. Your development as a grandparent is intimately linked to your grandchild's transition through the developmental cycle. It's important to keep in mind that every individual experiences each stage and makes each transition in a slightly different way. Also, the descriptions of ages and stages that follow are general guidelines, not hard and fast rules. One child may sleep a lot; another may be a fussy eater. One may be very verbal at an early age; another may begin to talk later. Some never go through the terrible twos, and others strain your patience to its limits. One grandchild may make the transition to school with comparative ease, while another experiences all kinds of difficulties.

Several studies also indicate that there are significant cultural differences in the ways children develop. As we'll see in our discussion of different models of grandparenting, comparisons across cultures teach us that there are *many* right ways to care for our children. Don't judge your grandchildren against a single ideal standard or try to measure them against each other.

Stage 1: The Infant, Zero to Eighteen Months

After you've gone through the experience of pregnancy and childbirth and the first days at home, your new grandchild, her parents, and you yourself will begin settling into a routine. The one thing your grandchild needs more than anything else during this period is a stable, consistent environment. In many cases, this is harder to provide than you might expect. Even for a relatively settled couple, the birth of their first child is an enormous transition. They've gone from a couple to a family, and their life has changed irrevocably. The spouse-lover is now also a father or a mother. The carefree days and spontaneity of their childless existence are over, and it can seem that life is dominated by feeding schedules and diapers. Just getting enough sleep becomes a major accomplishment, and finding quiet time alone becomes all but impossible.

During this first stage, the healthy infant develops what Erik Erikson has called "trust" but what others have called "confidence" or "security." Basically, it means that the baby begins to feel that the world he has come into is a good, safe, and predictable place. This most elementary form of trust evolves when his basic needs for food, warmth, and comfort are met. The infant is neither anxious nor angry when his mother moves out of sight, because he has an inner certainty that she will return.

One of the most important things to remember during this period is that there is no single correct way to love a baby. Babies are individuals and need different amounts and kinds of affection. Parents, too, have different ways of expressing their affection. Some are lavish with physical demonstrations of their feelings; others are less demonstrative. Some are soft and tender, others gruff and hardy. None of this matters very much so long as the parents' love shines through in a consistent and reliable form despite the inevitable variations and difficulties.

It is particularly important to keep this variety in mind when coming to the "proper" way to raise an infant. Scarcely a week goes by without some new report on the best way to

nurse, feed, lay in bed, put to sleep, and toilet train children. For example, after years of being told (usually by male "experts") that children should *never* be allowed to sleep with their parents, this orthodoxy has recently been challenged. Scores of parents need no longer feel guilty for taking their crying infant or toddler into their bed in order to get a good night's sleep! In fact, had we all been a little bit less narrow-minded, this would have been obvious long ago. Co-sleeping has long been the norm in well over half the societies in the world, including such diverse countries as Guatemala, Italy, and Japan.

Another good example is nursing. Many of today's grandparents were raised during the period when bottle-feeding and rigid scheduling (every four hours on the dot) were the norm. A U.S. Government publication from 1930 advised, "Feed him at exactly the same hours every day. Do not feed him just because he cries. Let him wait until the right time. If you make him wait, his stomach will learn to wait." Sleeping babies were awakened to get a bottle, and weaning was also done according to a very specific schedule. During the 1970s and 1980s, this model of formula-feeding was exported to parts of the Third World, often with disastrous results. Today, breast-feeding is more popular and nursing *on demand* more common. The majority of babies start with a three-hour schedule, move on to a four-hour schedule, and eventually settle in with four feedings a day.

The point of mentioning these examples (and I could provide many more) is to stress that you need to be very careful in offering advice. Just because you did things a certain way doesn't mean it's the only right way or even the way recommended by most pediatricians today. Most new parents,

especially those with a first child, are already anxious, confused, and exhausted. With little or no experience of a small baby to fall back upon, new parents worry when the baby cries and when quiet for too long. Many women are particularly anxious about breast-feeding, especially at the beginning. What they need from you more than anything else is reassurance, support, and, on occasion, some relief. Maybe it has been too long and you don't remember how overwhelming it can be to be totally responsible for a little human life for the first time. But if you think back, you will probably recall how important it was to you to know that you were doing a good job. The more confident and secure your grandchild's parent's feel, the easier it will be for them to pass those feelings on to their child.

Many women find the weeks and months after giving birth a period of emotional turmoil. A mother's happiness and contentment may be mixed with feelings of loss. Sometimes the very strength of her feelings for her new child seem to overwhelm her. These so-called baby blues are a common phenomenon and need not be a great concern. Indeed, one recent study suggests that this is a healthy, normal response. However, in about 10 or 15 percent of mothers, this depression after birth may be overwhelming, and your daughter or daughter-in-law may find that she is not coping. If you've never been through depression (this kind or any other), it's tempting to think that a simple pep talk or a Patton-like call to "Pull yourself together!" will solve everything. This is not the case.

Obviously, the father-husband needs to be the first line of support in such situations: supporting his wife while providing the stability and consistency that the baby needs. In many cases of postnatal (or postpartum) depression, the mother may

need professional coaching. With the intervention of the father and other supportive adults, the situation can usually be stabilized. Although you obviously have a responsibility to see that no harm comes to your grandchild, this is not an open invitation to take over. If your daughter or daughter-in-law is feeling depressed and inadequate, being told that she's an inadequate mother will not help her. It's usually much easier for the father to be supportive and provide mother and child what's needed. So tread carefully.

For valuable resources and reliable advice contact Depression after Delivery Information Request Line, P.O. Box 1282, Morrisville, PA 19067, 1-800-944-4PPD

Stage 2: The Toddler, Eighteen Months to Three Years

We all know how exhausting a toddler can be for both parents and grandparents. One of the best things you can do for your children is pinch-hit when they need it and your schedule permits. Of course, *you'll* also have to be in pretty good shape to hold your own with an active child. Don't be discouraged if your grandchild balks initially at being separated from her parents. Sometimes this will happen even if you are a regular visitor.

One of the most important lessons that your grandchild learns during this period is autonomy. She becomes aware of herself as a separate person and wants to do things for herself. The toddler demonstrates her autonomy and her desire for more of it by mastering her own body, including walking, climbing, jumping, and grabbing things and letting them go. She learns to control her bodily functions.

Toilet training is another of those areas that can drive parents nuts. Unfortunately, there always seem to be good reasons for parents to begin toilet training that have nothing to do with the child. In the nineteenth and early twentieth century, toilet training was begun very early, not only because there were no washing machines or disposable diapers, but also because it was believed that regularity was important to good health. In 1914, the U.S. Children's Bureau recommended that bowel training begin at three months or earlier! Though hardly anyone would suggest starting this early today, more and more parents feel pressured because they are sending their kids to day-care facilities that only accept children who are already out of diapers.

Unless you're willing to take over if your children don't find a day-care solution, you really can't say much about the toilet training schedule they choose. But you can help them maintain some perspective and a sense of humor. Remind them that everyone seems to get the hang of toilet training by the time they move on to other challenges—such as getting a driver's license, taking college entrance exams, or getting married!

The toddler's search for autonomy is enshrined in the folk wisdom concept of the terrible twos. Unlike the infant who expresses her discomfort by crying, the toddler makes her feelings felt far more directly. Since the child is now verbal, she can object with a resounding "no" to your suggestions. Since she is mobile, she can walk or run away when you call her or tell her to do something. For example, you may be trying to get home by a certain hour and you want her to sit in her stroller so you can get there as quickly as possible. She wants to walk and tells you so. You try to put her in the stroller and she squirms out as you try to buckle her in. It can just drive you crazy!

Although such behavior can try the patience of the most

saintly grandparent, it is important to appreciate such words and behavior for what they are: natural assertions of your grandchild's autonomy. And they do pass!

Stage 3: The Preschooler, Three to Seven Years

One of the most important things you can do with your grandchild during the preschool years is play. Play does not begin with the preschooler, of course; it starts much earlier, and ideally it should be a lifelong activity. But there are a few reasons for giving it special attention at this point in the child's development.

Although we haven't yet reached the extremes that one finds in some countries, it often seems that children are being asked to get serious earlier and earlier. Just as going to college was a significant achievement in my generation and getting into a good school was an important part of my children's high school experience, today we're seeing parents who want to be sure that their children get into the right preschool, kindergarten, or elementary school. Toy and game manufacturers have been quick to capitalize on this enthusiasm by developing specifically educational toys and slapping the label "educational" on almost anything they produce in the hope that it will attract more buyers.

It is certainly not my intention to criticize products or activities that prepare children for school. Even if my daughter Miriam weren't the president of HIPPY (Home Instruction Program for Preschool Youngsters), I would be an enthusiastic supporter of any program that promotes education by strengthening families and increasing the involvement of parents in their children's lives.

However, it sometimes seems that we get so involved in preparing children for formal school that we often forget just how valuable play is in this preparation. More than once I've been introduced to someone's precocious child or grandchild who has already been taught to read or do math or who has memorized the state capitals. Whether we're talking about formal games with specific rules to be learned and followed, competitive games with winners and losers, or just fooling around by dressing up and pretending, *never underestimate the importance of play*!

Stage 4: The Schoolchild and Preadolescent, Seven to Thirteen Years

Everyone has different preferences when it comes to "best age of all." But school age is certainly one of my favorites! At this age, your grandchildren are old enough to do lots of things on their own and young enough still to enjoy doing lots of things with you. It's a great age for going on trips, visiting places, and having your grandchildren come stay with you when they are on vacation.

Up to now, your grandchild's parents have been concerned mainly with establishing a daily routine and teaching your grandchildren the basics, such as how to dress, wash, and feed themselves. Parents of school-age children have a whole new set of issues, commonly including household chores, allowances, and just how much supervision is enough. Most of all, parents worry about how involved they should be in their child's schoolwork and what to do if there are academic, social, or behavioral problems.

With more and more children spending their preschool

years outside the home in some kind of day-care environment, the move into formal schooling is usually less dramatic than it was in the past. Nevertheless, it's a turning point in every child's and parent's life.

Although I've always felt that education should be a top priority, it is possible to put too much emphasis on academic achievements and, even more so, academic intelligence. The tasks demanded at school are in many ways different from those encountered in other settings: they are defined by other people and have little or no intrinsic interest to the learner. Such tasks, moreover, often have only a single correct answer and even a single correct way to reach that answer.

Recently a lot of attention has been given to the idea of *emotional* intelligence because of a best-selling book by that name. But some researchers have suggested that there are, in fact, many different kinds of intelligence, including:

Linguistic: sensitivity to language and nuances of words

Spatial: the ability to perceive relations between objects and to create and re-create images

Logical-mathematical: the ability to engage in abstract reasoning

Musical: sensitivity to pitch, tone, and musical structures

Bodily: the ability to represent ideas in movement such as dance and mime

Personal-Social: the ability to understand one's own feelings, motives, and behavior and those of others

One of our tasks as grandparents is to support our grandchildren as they explore all their abilities and skills. This is a wonderful age to attend a concert, go to a museum or basket-ball game, or take a hike. It's also the perfect time to encourage participation and experimentation. Trying out for Little League, joining a club or afterschool group, or picking up a musical instrument can all be loads of fun at this age. Of course, all of this needs to be done with the agreement of your grandchild's parents, but a well timed gift (see Chapter 8) of a tennis racket, chess set, or other active toy can work wonders at this age.

Stage 5: The Adolescent and Young Adult, Thirteen to Twenty-one Years

Although my grandchildren still have a number of years to go before they enter adolescence, teens and young adults are one of the groups that have a special place in my heart. College students are just about my favorite audience, and I try to lecture to them as often as I can. By talking to teens and young adults, I keep my finger on the pulse of the next generation, and their questions are always a source of amusement, amazement, and enlightenment.

Many of the physical and psychological changes undergone by today's adolescents are no different from those you or I experienced when it was our turn. But today's teens and young adults are also facing some circumstances that are different from those of any previous generation. The women's movement, the pill, AIDS, and gay liberation are only some of them. Consider the following: In 1991, more teens and young adults died from suicide than from cancer, heart disease, AIDS, pneumonia, influenza, and lung disease combined. In 1992 alone, more than 450,000 teens were cited for drunk driving. That same year, 365,000 unwed teenagers became mothers. Every day, 135,000 children take guns to school. And average combined scores on the Scholastic Aptitude Test have dropped 78 points since 1963.

The process of growing from a child into an adult is never a smooth one, and it's good to remember just how tumultuous it can be. Whether you're the first one to grow breasts or a mustache or the last, your body never seems just right. Take it from me: I stopped growing at 4 feet 7 inches, and it caused me a lot of pain until I resolved never to let my height (or lack of it) stop me.

The physical changes your teenage grandson or granddaughter is undergoing are small change compared to the emotional turmoil. Adolescence is a period of new friendships, peer pressure, and a whole new set of feelings. It's also a period of firsts: first car, first date, first kiss, first orgasm, and maybe first sexual intercourse.

Although I suppose it's natural that I should place a great deal of emphasis on the sexual development of teens and young adults (old habits die hard!), this is only one part of the evolution of an adult identity. Adolescence is also the period when many people begin to forge an independent political, religious, and ethnic identity.

As if all these changes weren't enough, adolescence and young adulthood is also a period of major readjustments within the family unit. Conflicts between adolescents and parents can arise on almost any issue: dating, sex, friendships, dress, chores, money, cars, school, manners, politics, and on and on. Such conflicts are an almost inevitable part of the adolescent's learning to become independent and defining himself as an individual and not just a member of his family.

All of this makes grandparenting a real challenge. Although it is often claimed that the reason grandparents and grandchildren get along so well is that they have a common enemy, this is far from the norm and is certainly not an ideal. One of the most important things for you to do during this period is maintain your balance. Both your children and your grandchildren need your support, and you can only provide it if you keep the larger picture in mind and don't take sides on every issue. Being supportive doesn't mean approving of everything they do. It *does* mean being nonjudgmental and always reminding both parents and child how much you cherish them.

Most teenagers experiment with new things and test themselves and those around them. Inevitably some get into trouble. One thing that those who get through these difficulties have in common is support from those who love them.

Your grandchild's transition into adolescence often marks a watershed in his or her relationship with parents and grandparents. If the stereotypical picture of the grandparent is the elderly, feeble homebody of "Little Red Riding Hood," the complementary picture of the grandchild usually ranges only from infant to pre-teen.

Although your grandchildren are far more *capable* of initiating contact during this period in their lives, this doesn't mean that you should sit back and wait for them to reach out to you. Teens are busy and self-involved. From age eighteen on they may be away at college. Don't be shy. Pick up the phone or send an e-mail, a letter, or a present.

As your grandchild becomes a teenager, it may not be only the amount of time you spend with your grandchild that changes. The nature of the relationship will be transformed as well. For grandparents who live near their grandchildren, teenage grandchildren often provide important assistance by running errands or helping with household chores. For many years it may have been the grandparent who helped out by chauffeuring. The late teen not only no longer needs this assistance, but may be called upon to help an older grandparent get to the store, the doctor, or a club or other activities. For example, one study found that grandchildren aged eighteen to twenty-four often give their grandparents gifts (96 percent), shop or run errands (84 percent), help out at times of illness (81 percent), take them places (69 percent), and fix things around the house (65 percent).

Stage 6: Adulthood, When Grandchildren Are No Longer Children

Teacher: How many of you have great-grandparents?

Yona (age 3): All my grandparents are great!

Adulthood is, of course, a far longer phase than any of the others discussed in this chapter. If this were a longer book or one dealing with a slightly different topic, I might have lots to say about the many changes this stage involves. Here, I have to limit myself to a few points.

It may seem like only yesterday that your children were finishing school, finding jobs, and marrying. It can't possibly be that your grandchildren are already adults and that your children are now the proud grandparents!

At the beginning of this century, most grandparents did not live to see their grandchildren enter into adulthood, marry, and raise a family. Grandparents of adult grandchildren were comparatively rare and great-grandparents even rarer. This has changed dramatically in this century. Indeed, great-grandparenthood can be said to occupy much the same niche today as grandparenthood did a century ago: not all that common and little understood. In fact, if the twentieth century saw the emergence of grandparenthood as a distinct phase in the life cycle, there is every reason to believe that the twenty-first century will see the same thing happen for great-grandparents. Doubtless this will also produce a wave of studies of great-grandparents and their relationships with their adult grandchildren. For the time being, this subject remains rather understudied.

Based on the limited literature available, there are indications that adult grandchildren are often closer to their grandparents than adolescents. It appears that as they settle into jobs, marry, and begin to raise their own families, their appreciation of and concern with intergenerational family ties grow. Of course, there are often practical barriers. Adult grandchildren and great-grandchildren are more likely to live far away than children and younger grandchildren.

Age is another real consideration in this case. Although it's wonderful to be at the top of the family tree—and sometimes the view is breathtaking—the heights can make it much more difficult to nurture all the branches and roots. By the time your grandchildren are adults, you are probably long on perspective but you may be much shorter on energy.

This is certainly a time to treasure. Even if your contacts with large part of your family are limited to special occasions like holidays and birthday parties, there is something marvelous about being surrounded by a roomful of your descendants. It gives you a good sense of the mark you've made on the world, the legacies you've managed to pass on, and the bridges to the future you've managed to construct.

Further Reading

COLE, MICHAEL and SHEILA. *The Development of Children*, 3rd ed. (New York: W.H. Freeman and Company, 1996).

ERIKSON, ERIK, H. *Childhood and Society* (New York: W.W. Norton, 1963).

———. *Identity: Youth and Crises* (New York: W.W. Norton, 1968).

Created in Our Own Image: Choosing Our Grandparenting Style

The Better to See You With: The Power of Myths

Once upon a time, at the edge of a large forest there stood a tiny cottage almost hidden by the trees. In it a little girl lived with her mother. The little girl could often be seen, in her red hood and cape, flitting among the tall trees. Her grandmother had made the hood and cape for her. Because the little girl always wore them, she was called Little Red Riding Hood.

One morning Little Red Riding Hood's mother packed a basket with some homemade chocolate cake, a jar of strawberry jam and a bottle of creamy milk. "Take this basket to your grandmother, Little Red Riding Hood. She is sick in bed, and this food will do her good. Besides, she will be happy to see you."

The classic children's story "Little Red Riding Hood" contains almost all the main features of one stereotyped image of a grandparent. Red Riding Hood's grandmother is old and feeble, caring and gift-giving, and lives within convenient walking distance (wolves notwithstanding) of her granddaughter.

There are probably some grandparents who fit this image. There are probably even more who wish they matched some parts of it. But in today's world, many grandparents are neither old nor feeble. They don't eat chocolate cake or drink creamy milk, especially when they're sick. Their lives are focused not on their grandchildren but on their jobs, friends, and social activities. Often they live not on the other side of the woods but on the other side of the country, on another continent, or at least somewhere where the winters are milder and the weather is sunnier.

One of the things I learned from the work I've done both with families and about sex is just how powerful myths are. In the area of family life, it's striking to see how many people cling to idealized images from the past. There's certainly nothing wrong with having romantic and nostalgic ideas, but if we walk around feeling that our lives are only second best because things were once much better, it can sap all our strength. And if we invest our energy in trying to live the way we imagine people used to live, we're bound to be disappointed.

Nowhere is this truer than in the case of grandparenting. As I've already discussed, the dismay that some people feel upon becoming grandparents is directly connected to their (mistaken) assumption that grandparents look and act like old people. Small wonder that most of those in their fifties or early sixties aren't ready to abandon their full and fulfilling lives for knitting and the rocking chair.

They often have few other models to fall back on, however.

Of all the roles in the nuclear and extended family, none is as loosely defined as that of the grandparent. Fairy tales notwithstanding, no single dominant model exists of what a grandparent is supposed to do and how a grandparent is supposed to act. Some authorities on family dynamics have described the grandparental role as vague, ambiguous, roleless, or even empty. What's certain is that many grandparents, especially first-timers, are often left unsure of what is expected of them and how best to fill their role.

At least one reason for the comparative dearth of grandparenting models is that grandparenting as a separate stage in the life cycle is relatively new. In the not too distant past, many grandparents were still raising their youngest children when their first grandchildren arrived. In 1900, about half of all fifty-year-old women had children under age eighteen at home. (Contrary to the common perception that women married at an early age in the past, the median age at first marriage for American women in the 1890s was around twenty-two.) For these women, grandparenting was a secondary role. Only when the last child had left home did it become their focus. For them, being a grandmother was not a distinct phase in their lives but, except for a comparatively brief period, a supplement to parenting.

By 1980 (although the median age of marriage, after a decline, had once again risen to twenty-two), only a quarter of fifty-year-old women had children at home. Many of these women defined their family position (after a period of having neither children at home nor grandchildren) first and foremost as grandmothers. Moreover, because they were living so much longer than in the first half of the century, the grandparenting phase might last two or three decades or more. In short, grandparenting has developed as an independent role in the family cycle and often extends as long or longer than parenting.

In choosing a grandparenting style, it is probably most important to ask yourself some key questions:

What kinds of things do I enjoy doing?

What special skills do I have?

How much time do I have available and how much do I want to spend grandparenting?

What are my children's and grandchildren's needs?

What religious and ethnic traditions do I want to pass on to my grandchildren?

Even today, when grandparenthood is much more defined as a part of the life cycle, there are still no set definitions of a good grandparent—any more than of a good grandchild. In this chapter, I will not tell you what kind of grandparent you *should* be but will present some of the options and some of the keys to being the best grandparent you *can* be. Far from being empty or vague, I believe the grandparent role to be open, dynamic, and flexible. If there's no consensus as to what a grandparent *should* be, so much the better! It just makes it all the easier for each of us to reinvent grandparenting in our own image for our own family.

Some Basic Styles

Over the years, scholars have made numerous attempts to classify the different types of grandparents. There is no widespread agreement on the best way to make the division. One attempt that I've found very interesting was proposed by Berniece Neugarten and Karol Weinstein in their now-classic 1964 article, "The Changing American Grandparent." Based on interviews with grandparents rather than on a theoretical model, they were able to identify five basic styles:

Fun-seeking

Formal

Distant

Reservoirs of family wisdom

Surrogate parents

By their own admission, Neugarten and Weinstein were interested in describing each grandparent's predominant style rather than all the different roles they filled. Many grandparents combine elements of each of these types, and some more recent studies have tried to reflect this complexity.

It also has to be remembered that thirty-five years is an enormous time in the study of grandparents. Many of the grandchildren of 1964 are today fast approaching or have already begun grandparenthood. There is no reason to assume that your style will fit those found among your grandparents. The baby boom of the 1950s meant that many grandparents of that period had lots of grandchildren to keep them busy and interested. Today, you are far more likely to have a smaller number of grandchildren—even only one or two. Obviously, being at the top of a beanpole is very different from being at the top of a pyramid.

You may find that your grandparenting style changes over time as your circumstances change and your grandchildren grow. So take the models that follow as general guides, not as goals to be achieved.

The *fun-seeking* (or what some have called *companionate*) grandparent's relationship to his grandchildren is marked especially by informality and playfulness. He joins the child in specific activities with the express purpose of having fun, almost as if he were a playmate. Being with the grandchildren is viewed as a sort of leisure activity or as a source of self-indulgence. The relationship is one in which authority lines—either with the grandchild or with the parent—are irrelevant. The emphasis here is on mutual satisfaction rather than on providing treats for the grandchild.

Neugarten and Weinstein found this to be the most common grandparenting style among those under sixty-five. Although they believe this changes as the grandparents themselves grow older, others suggest that the changes in style reflect changes in the age of the grandchildren. It's just a lot harder to have this kind of relationship with a teenager than it is with a baby or small child.

Fun-seeking grandparents seem to put an emphasis on their grandchildren's social lives and relationships. They are most interested in their friendships, how they get along with other children, and whether they are considerate of others.

One of the things that makes this style particularly interesting is that we find little evidence that it existed as a grandparenting style until comparatively recently. Very few grandparents interviewed in the 1960s and 1970s remembered their own grandparents as playful. Nor does this fun-seeking grandparent appear prominently in many traditional cultures. In short, it seems to be a modern invention.

Formal grandparents are those who follow what they regard as the proper and traditionally prescribed role for grandparents. Although they like to provide special treats and indulgences for their grandchildren and may occasionally provide minor assistance to the parents such as baby-sitting, they make sure there is a clear difference between parenting and grandparenting. They leave parenting strictly to the parents. They are very interested in the grandchild but are careful not to offer advice on childrearing. Neugarten and Weinstein found this to be the most common style among grandparents over age sixty-five. It seems to be a style more appropriate to older grandchildren than the fun-seeking style.

It is not surprising that formal grandparents have the same expectations of "proper" behavior from their grandchildren as they have for themselves. They put an emphasis on good manners, neatness and cleanliness, and self-control.

Consider this testimony from a French-American family:

> The way that my grandfather was, all the time I was growing up, I never remember him playing with the grandchildren at all. When we sat at the table it was always, "Now don't you wiggle the table because your grandfather will yell at you." He had his own special things that you couldn't touch. You couldn't go in his room. Children were to be seen and not heard. That's the way it was, and everyone was very respectful to him.

The *distant* grandparent emerges from the shadows on holidays and on special occasions such as graduations and birthdays. Unlike the formal grandparent, the distant grandparent's contact with his grandchild is fleeting and infrequent. This grandparent is benevolent in stance but essentially distant and remote.

Before I say anymore about the distant grandparent, I must make a very important clarification. Although distant grandparents are often those who live at a great distance, researchers agree: *geography is not destiny*! It is, to be sure, much easier to maintain a close relationship if you live nearby, but as I'll discuss in Chapter 6, there are lots of ways to keep in touch and up-to-date even if you live far away. There are plenty of grandparents who live within a few miles of their grandchildren but have adopted a distant style.

The *reservoir of family wisdom* represents a distantly authoritarian relationship in which the grandparent—almost always the grandfather—is the dispenser of special skills or resources. Lines of authority are distinct, and the young parents maintain and emphasize their subordinate position—sometimes without resentment. These grandparents put an emphasis on such virtues as honesty, common sense, and responsibility.

A number of years ago, I spent a Fourth of July weekend with a family whose grandfather exemplified this role. During the course of the weekend, his wife, acting as a sort of appointments secretary, made sure that each of his three daughters, their husbands, and all of his more than a dozen grandchildren had time to talk with him alone. He updated himself on everyone's activities and usually concluded each conversation with a statement of approval or disapproval, a recommendation regarding the future, and, when relevant, the name of a friend or acquaintance who might be of some help. As far as I could tell, none of the parents (all of them successful professionals in their own right) questioned his right to advise his grandchildren on matters including study habits, choice of a musical instrument, selection of a college or graduate school, or job prospects. Although it was a little too reminiscent of the opening scene of *The Godfather* for my taste, it seemed to work admirably for this family.

Some grandparents find themselves in the role of *surrogate parents*. This style of grandparenting appears almost exclusively among women. It usually occurs in situations when the young mother works and the grandmother assumes the actual caretaking responsibility for the child. One New York schoolteacher I know had this situation with each of her four children. Every morning she dressed her preschoolers and, on her way to work, dropped them off with her mother, who lived nearby. Grandma fed them breakfast and, weather permitting, took them to a park or some other activity. After lunch they had a nap and played some more until either their mother or father came to pick them up. If for some reason the parents were delayed, grandma fed them supper as well.

According to the Department of Commerce, 62 percent of preschoolers in poor families are cared for by relatives while their mothers work. In 1996, more than 1.9 million children were living with their mothers in the homes of their grandparents. In some cases, as I shall discuss in Chapter 12, this style can evolve into a situation in which the grandparent is actually filling all parental roles, either temporarily or permanently.

It is not surprising that this type of grandparent holds expectations that are very similar to those of many parents: try hard, obey your elders, be a good student. As the name indicates, the line between parenting and grandparenting is blurred in these cases, with little or no formal separation of responsibilities.

A Special Word about the Roles of Grandfathers

*There are fathers who do not love their children,
there is no grandfather who does not adore his grandson*

Victor Hugo

When I was discussing this book with my editors, one of the dilemmas I faced was whether or not I should include a separate section on grandfathers and, if so, if I had to include a similar section on grandmothers.

The arguments for giving special attention to grandfathers are pretty straightforward. First and foremost, grandfathers have generally received far less attention than grandmothers. Although there are numerous useful books such as *Becoming a Grandmother, The Grandmother Book*, and *Bubbe and Gram: My Two Grandmothers*, there are far fewer books directed solely to grandfathers. (A notable recent exception is Charlton Heston's *To Be a Man: Letters to My Grandson*, which I hope is a sign of things to come.) So I felt that some special attention to grand-*fathers* might be a useful bit of affirmative action.

Second, most studies indicate that gender is one of the most important variables in determining the roles grandparents play. Although the data on this subject are far more limited than the data for mothers and fathers, certain trends are evident. Grandfathers are usually the ones to be *reservoirs of family wisdom;* grandmothers are the most common *surrogate parents.* Grandfathers are more likely to act as "secretaries of state," keeping an eye on the family's dealings with the larger world: schools, jobs, and legal matters. Grandmothers tend to fill the role of "ministers of the interior," tending to relationships within the family both within and between the

generations. Grandmothers often put more emphasis on affection and caring, while grandfathers frequently worry about
finances, education, and employment. Finally, grandfathers are
apt to treat their grandsons far differently than granddaughters, while grandmothers are prone to draw fewer distinctions.

These differences between grandfathering and grandmoth-
ering would be in and of themselves reason enough for devoting some special attention to grandfathers, but there is
another consideration as well. The role of *fathers* has changed
dramatically over the past generation. Traditionally, fathers
were more or less distant, authoritarian figures whose tempers
always had to be feared (remember "Wait till your father gets
home?") and who, except for an occasional outing, left child
care and nurturing to mom.

Even in the midst of this very long tradition, however, there
were some wonderful, nurturing fathers. From 1988 to 1991,
the percentage of fathers who were the primary caregivers for
preschoolers shot up from 15 to 20 percent. During the same
period, the percentage of unmarried fathers who cared for
their children rose from 1.5 to 7 percent. Although some of
these changes appear to reflect short-term economic realities
rather than long-term shifts in family patterns, they are wor-
thy of comment.

Even in cases where the father isn't the primary caregiver,
things have changed significantly during the past twenty-five
years. A nationwide survey of fathers found that 81 percent
reported taking a bigger part in child-care duties than their
fathers had, 68 percent spend more time with their children,
and 44 percent believe their children know them better as a
person than they knew their fathers. If these figures are even
remotely accurate (some researchers believe that because of

new social norms, men frequently exaggerate the actual amount of time they spend with their children), it means that today's fathers have a much more intense parenting experience than today's grandfathers had. In other words, a major generation gap has developed, and new grandfathers may find themselves seriously lacking in child-care experience.

Unfortunately, involved fathers are only one part of the changes that have taken place in fatherhood over the past three decades. While many dads are playing a far greater role in their children's lives, another group of fathers has all but dropped out. Between 1970 and 1994, the percentage of children living in single-parent households headed by their mothers more than doubled, from 11 percent to 23 percent. Although much has been written about black matriarchal households (over half of all African-American households are headed by women), the rise has been steeper among whites, for whom the numbers have shot up from 8 percent in 1970 to 18 percent in 1994.

Despite heroic efforts by millions of mothers and grandmothers, there is a grim result of this lack of contact. Studies show that the absence of the father (or some other male role model, *such as a grandfather,* who's a regular part of their lives) can have direct adverse effects in boys, particularly if the separation from the father occurs before age five. In our culture, it is the fathers who have traditionally been expected to exert discipline and to provide examples of when aggression is appropriate or inappropriate. When the fathers are absent, these issues are often unresolved. Studies indicate that fatherlessness is an indicator of delinquency, poor test scores, substance abuse, and other problems. Some 70 percent of long-term prisoners in penal institutions in the United States are men who grew up without fathers. And fatherlessness afflicts girls, too. A positive, loving, trusting relationship with a father is a model for how they will eventually relate to males in general. Girls who live in single-parent homes (which are overwhelmingly single mother homes) experience 111 percent more teenage births, 164 percent more premarital births, and 92 percent more marital breakups than those from two-parent households.

One clear conclusion to be drawn from all this is that given the large number of households that have no father present, grandfathers have a vital role to play in modern family life. In saying this, it is not my intention to belittle the heroic efforts made by the countless women who are daily called upon to be both father and mother to their children. (Grandmothers obviously have a similar complementary role to play in the 3 to 4 percent of father-only households.) Nor am I suggesting that the government can ignore its obligations to our nation's children by passing the responsibility onto grandparents.

What I am suggesting, however, is that our current reality demands a serious rethinking of *grandfatherhood*. Given the realities of modern family life (and I'll have much more to say about this in Chapter 9), it's time we stop thinking of grandfathers as either passive figures or distant judges. Perhaps the most important role for grandfathers to play today is that of models—models of warm, caring, concerned, and involved men who can serve as a vital reminder that *real men care for their families.*

5

Vital Roles

vital: *adj.* of or pertaining to life; being the seat or source of life; necessary to the existence, continuance, or well-being of something; indispensable, essential; of critical importance

In the last chapter, I discussed some of the different styles of grandparenting. We saw that grandparenting is still a comparatively underdefined role and that the basic types of grandparents defined by most researchers offer only a rough picture of a complex and ever-changing reality.

Looking at grandparenting styles is only one way to understand the vital roles we play in the lives of our grandchildren. Another way to understand the ways we grandparent is to distinguish between the *instrumental* and *symbolic* tasks we perform. The instrumental tasks include all the practical assistance grandparents provide their children and grandchildren: child care, financial support, and, in some cases, housing. Although there are important exceptions, most American parents prefer to minimize the instrumental role of grandparents. Given the opportunity, they seek to be independent and draw clear lines between parenting, which includes their children's daily needs, and grandparenting, which is more sporadic and more symbolic. Despite these efforts and this ideal, there is clear evidence that grandparents continue to provide important practical assistance, whether through financial support or gifts (Chapter 8). Moreover, at times of crises such as divorce (Chapter 11), grandparents' instrumental tasks increase, sometimes to the point of assuming primary responsibility for their grandchildren (Chapter 12).

Despite these examples, the general trend over the past century or more has been for grandparents to focus increasingly on the symbolic aspects of their role. In other words, grandparents are concentrating less on what they do for their families and more on what they *mean* to their families.

Although it might be easy to conclude from this that grandparents are less important than in the past, I think precisely the opposite may be true. If anything, grandparents are more *vital* than ever before. Although our families may not need our help on a daily practical level, this doesn't mean that all their needs are being met. Countless books and authors have commented on the development of lifestyles that are full of things but empty of meaning. As grandparents, we are in a unique position to provide some of the things that money just can't buy: continuity, trust, stability, love, understanding, and unconditional support. In fact, far from being superfluous in today's world, we have not one but several indispensable roles to fill in the lives of our grandchildren.

It would take me several books to discuss all the ways in which involved grandparents are essential to the existence, continuance, and well-being of the modern family, so I've decided to focus on only five: historian, model, teacher, confidant, and safety net.

Family Historian Making the Past Real

One good grandmother went a long way with her stories, her store of old fashioned songs, and her vanishing skills in making gingerbread men and cookies. With these pleasures children absorbed a sense of the past, could measure time in meaningful biological terms, when grandmother was young, when mother was young, when I was young. Dates became real instead of contentless numbers in a history book, and progress, measured by steamships, telegraph, and automobiles, could be related to the pictures of grandmother and grandfather as bride and groom, or as pater-familias with a parent and aunts and uncles in a family picture.

Margaret Mead

Although books can certainly convey what a particular time period was like, you get a much clearer picture from real people, especially people you love. I feel very lucky that I've been able to publish my autobiography and that the Arts and Entertainment Network has included a show about me in its "Biography" series. Both of my children have read the book and have seen the show, and I look forward to sharing them with my grandchildren when they're old enough to appreciate them.

Even if you can't publish a book, you can share your history and that of your family with your grandchildren by writing your memoirs for your children and grandchildren. If writing is not your style, you can sit down and tape your stories. One family I know took advantage of their father-grandfather's eightieth birthday for just such a purpose. They all knew that he would, when asked, share his reminiscences of his life in Poland, Austria, and Germany, as well as his migration to the United States and his fifty years teaching history at Columbia University. Well armed with tape recorders and plenty of batteries, they were able to preserve his stories for future generations. Several families I know have moved one step up the technological ladder and have made videotapes of their family history.

Ever since the publication of Alex Haley's bestseller *Roots* and the subsequent miniseries, many institutions have become involved in tracing family stories. Schools often have projects in which students explore their roots. Research has shown that such projects strengthen young people's understanding of their heritage and build ties between them and older members of their family. Significantly, students who have participated in such projects have found that they not only opened the door for future communication with their grandparents but also promoted a better understanding of their parents.

Even if you don't get involved in any single project to tell your story, you will have many opportunities to share your history. I know that neither my book nor my tape contains more than a small fraction of the stories I've told my children over the years about Germany, their grandparents, and life in Israel. Next time you're asked, "Grandma, tell me a story," why not skip "The Three Little Pigs" and "Little Red Riding Hood" and tell one of your own stories.

Remember that the meaning and details of your story that matter the most will differ with the age of your grandchildren. Some stories are best told a little at a time, bit by bit, with new details and incidents recounted as your grandchildren get old enough to appreciate them. And never forget that even the most fascinating story can lose its attraction after many repetitions.

Serving as a family historian is not limited to storytelling. When Steve's daughter Yona had her twelfth birthday, her grandmother gave her a photo album tracing the family history from the time she arrived in the United States from Germany in 1939 to the present. Each picture had a short explanation identifying the people and giving some of the historical background. She also left the album half empty, for the story continues.

There are also several excellent ready-made books that you can use to tell your story, such as *Grandfather/Grandmother Remembers: Memories for My Grandchild* and *Grandmother's Precious Moments, Special Memories for My Grandchild.* All you have to do is fill in the facts or paste in the pictures at the appropriate place and you have a marvelous gift for your grandchild.

The role of family historian need not be limited to large projects or complicated traditions. It may also mean passing down a particular recipe to your grandchildren or an especially beloved melody of a lullaby. It may also involve handing down a special holiday tradition or making copies of a special picture. At the entrance to his apartment, Steve has a picture that shows him (as a baby), his father, grandfather, and great-grandfather in front of a building on New York's Lower East Side. It captures both a brief moment in family history and a story. Each generation of adult males is dressed a little less traditionally and a little more "American." Like so many good pictures, it tells the story of a family in an immediate and personal manner.

As a family historian, you are your children's and grandchildren's bridge to the past and they are your link with immortality.

Model: Leading by Example

The mature person is one of the most remarkable products that any
society can bring forth. He or she is a living cathedral,
the handiwork of many individuals over many years.

David W. Plath, *Long Engagements: Maturity in Modern Japan*

One of the greatest gifts you can give to your grandchildren is providing a model that they can learn from and emulate. Modeling is a multifaceted role. It takes place on a daily basis and also in connection with certain specific aspects of life. It is a crucial supplement (and some would say prelude) to the next role I shall discuss, that of teacher. Many of the most valuable lessons we learn in life are based not on theory or explanation but on examples. Indeed, there are few influences more powerful than the lives lived by those we love, respect, and admire.

One vital model that we grandparents can provide concerns our pride in our own ethnic or religious heritage. As a family historian or teacher, you may pass on a particular recipe, melody, custom, or other skill. But on a daily basis, you can demonstrate what it means to live your faith or represent your people in the world. Different cultures have developed special ways of being and treating a grandparent. In fact, whatever your background, there is no better example of the full meaning of your heritage than the way it guides your life. Whether it's the way you treat your coworkers or employers, the respect you show to your traditions and those of others, or the charities to which you give both time and money, your example provides your grandchildren with a vision of their birthright that may stick with them throughout their lives.

As a grandparent you also have an opportunity to model healthy parent-child relations. We all know families in which generation after generation is involved in feuds, disputes, and other recriminations. Sometimes it even reaches the point where parents and children or other family members stop speaking to each other altogether. There are many causes behind such multigenerational feuds, but at least one reason that they seem to be hereditary is that children learn family behaviors from their parents and grandparents. There are few more meaningful messages to hand down than modeling effective communication with those you love most.

Modeling often comes to the fore in difficult times. Whether it's a momentary setback or a family crisis such as a serious illness or divorce, your children and grandchildren will probably look to you for guidance in how to respond. To paraphrase Kipling, if you can keep your head when all around you are losing theirs, you'll set a fine example.

Teacher: A Life of Lessons

The elderly are a treasure in the household.

Chinese proverb

Perhaps the oldest of all roles for grandparents is that of the teacher, passing on the knowledge and experiences they've gained during their lives. Before formal education became widespread in the United States and elsewhere in the world, grandparents and other elders were great repositories of wisdom and life experience for the younger generations. Recent studies of African-American grandparents indicate that they score particularly high in teaching their grandchildren sensitivity to the feelings of others, good manners, a sense of right and wrong, and the need to continue learning throughout life.

Today, despite certain trends toward home schooling, we have passed much of the responsibility for this outside the family. But there are still many opportunities to teach your grandchildren, for all of us have skills and talents to share. Whatever your particular passion—playing chess, crocheting, baseball, or backgammon—you can teach it to your grandchildren in a way that no professional teacher, instructional video, or how-to book can. Not only do you get the pleasure of the teaching itself and sharing your enthusiasm over a particular hobby, but often you will develop a basis for many common experiences in the future. One friend of mine convinced her grandmother to teach her to speak Russian, and for years, until the grandmother's recent death at age ninety, it was "their" language.

One of the most important things you can teach your grandchildren is how to be a good teacher. Explain and share with patience and understanding, imparting not only the dry facts and how-to's, but also the fun and the joy you find in pursuing your vocation or hobbies. You may also have the opportunity to benefit directly from this particular lesson when your grandchildren teach you.

In my experience, all my best teachers were also good students, not only in the sense that they did well in school but that they combined a love of learning with their teaching. This is true for grandparents as well.

I've already discussed how important it is to keep an open mind about the way your grandchildren are being raised, asking questions before and usually *instead of* giving advice. This is also important with your grandchildren.

Although your grandchildren may not have the kind of wisdom you've developed over the years, they often have information and skills that can benefit you. This is obvious in almost anything connected to computers, which are becoming more and more common everyday. In the case of older children, it may also be true with regard to car mechanics, travel arrangements, and educational opportunities. For many young people, especially teens, just the fact that you respect their opinion and value what they know will win you lots of points. It shows you're not just treating them like a kid and that you've paid attention as they've grown and matured.

Do not be afraid to boldly go where you have never gone before. If you expect your grandchildren to at least try opera, ballet, or Indian cooking, or to accompany you to an exhibition of Impressionist art, there's no reason why you shouldn't take a chance and learn about their favorite music group, accompany them to a film, learn a little about macrobiotic cooking, or visit a crafts fair. You may surprise yourself!

Confidant

Trust is vital to any relationship, and hopefully your grandchildren and their parents share talk frequently and openly. However, there will be times when children, particularly teenagers, want to confide in an adult other than their parents. It may be a teacher, coach, or school counselor—or it may be a *grandparent*.

Trust does not suddenly emerge out of thin air, however. It's built up slowly over the years, step by step. If every time your grandson confides in you, you pass the information on to his parents, don't be surprised if his confidence in you soon fades. I'm not suggesting that you lie to his parents or hide the fact that he is involved in something illegal or dangerous. But as anyone else, your grandchild has the right to privacy and to believe that his confidences will be respected. Such trust can pay major dividends at times of family crises such as illness or divorce. Your grandson may not want to share his fears, anger, or confusion with his parents. Having someone close to turn to can be a blessing in such circumstances. Moreover, the situation need not necessarily be so dramatic.

Consider the case of a boy I know named Geoffrey. One of his closest friends, Paul, lived on the same block. From an early age, Paul and Geoffrey were inseparable. When they started junior high, Paul went to a different school, and a few months later Geoffrey found out that he was smoking marijuana. Paul and Geoffrey continued to see each other, but Geoffrey was concerned for his friend and resented Paul's pressuring him to try pot as well.

Geoffrey thought of going to his parents to discuss his dilemma, but he was afraid they would insist he stop seeing Paul. Even worse, since Geoffrey's parents were friends of Paul's parents, he thought they might go to them, and he didn't want to betray his friend. Still, Geoffrey wanted the advice of an adult, so he went to his grandfather, who lived nearby and with whom he had a close relationship.

Geoffrey asked his grandfather to promise that he wouldn't tell his mom and dad, and when his grandfather was assured that Geoffrey was not involved with drugs, he agreed. Geoffrey told his grandfather the whole story. Geoffrey's grandfather suggested that he and other friends of Paul get together and promise one another to stay away from drugs and to try to stop Paul as well. Geoffrey felt relieved on all counts. Because he could trust his grandfather, he was able to discuss his problem with an adult and even got useful advice on how to proceed.

One thing that this story shows is that sometimes your greatest achievement may go almost unnoticed. The proverbial ounce of prevention is often greatly underestimated. As your grandchild's confidant, you may spare him and your whole family a great deal of anxiety. Sometimes this can be more valuable than any more visible gift you have to give.

Safety Net

As we've already seen, family and community life in the past were neither as peaceful nor as perfect as we have been taught to believe. Idealized portraits of serene rural homesteads or beloved elders growing old in comfort and with dignity probably teach us more about our own dreams than about our forebears' lives.

Whatever the truth about the past, it is significant that the past is remembered as a period of more gradual change and much greater stability. Even if this is not the case, our nostalgic memory says a lot about our own longing for a less tumultuous existence. Not only does everything seem to be changing before our eyes these days, but change itself seems to be happening at a faster and faster pace.

In a world of jet travel, instant communication, and global culture, is it any wonder that children grow up feeling that they can be anywhere in an instant but have nowhere that's their special place? With high divorce rates, youth gangs, and beauty pageants for five-year-olds robbing more and more children of their childhood, what better role to fill than that of an island of stability in a sea of change?

In a world of runaway change, grandparents have a vital role to play in providing security and consistency. This doesn't mean, that you can't continue to grow and change. It does mean, however, that whatever changes take place in your life, your grandchildren always know they can depend on you.

Always remember that being a safety net does not mean fostering dependence. Just as the circus trapeze artist can take all sorts of chances and attempt amazing tricks because she knows she has a safety net, you want to give your grandchildren that same freedom to dare. No one goes to the circus to watch a performer hold on to a tent pole, terrified that she might fall.

One of the most important lessons you can teach your grandchildren is the difference between a problem and a crisis. One of the things that I've noticed about myself and many of my peers whose lives were horribly disrupted during World War II is that this experience gave us an important lesson in the difference between real crises—war, unexpected death, serious illness—and the usual challenges that life throws in everyone's way. Teaching your grandson that he can depend on you also means teaching him to know that he can depend on himself.

Throughout the second half of the twentieth century, China has been racked by major turmoil on several occasions, most notably the Communist revolution of 1949 and the Cultural Revolution of the 1960s. In the latter case, the authorities fostered the formation of "grandma families" to ease the burdens created by the disintegration of traditional families.

Although this safety net role often comes to the fore in times of crisis, like any other part of successful grandparenting, it doesn't just happen. Just as becoming your grandchild's confidant depends on building trust over the years, being the person he turns to in time of need is the result of many smaller interventions in which you've listened well and lent a shoulder to cry on or a sympathetic ear.

Your Own Role

The roles discussed in this chapter are only a sampling of the special positions you may have in the lives of your grandchildren. Each of your grandchildren is different and their needs may vary. However much you may have enjoyed being the confidant of one, do not let that get in the way of teaching another valuable lessons or giving another a sense of the richness of her family's history. Remember that it is always you who defines the role you play, based on the circumstances and the type of relationship you have with each grandchild and his parents. Don't let yourself get typecast into one particular position. Be ready to grow, change, and explore.

6

Distance Is Only Relative, Especially If You're the Relative

The Myth of the Three-Generation Household

One of the most popular misconceptions about family life in the past is that most children grew up in three-generation households alongside their parents and grandparents. Recent research has conclusively dispelled this myth. In the American colonies and preindustrial Europe, the presence of grandparents, parents, and grandchildren in the same household was *not* the normal family arrangement.

First of all, there were just too many grandchildren and too few grandparents for this to be a very common situation. A typical family looked like a pyramid with many more (younger) members at the base, and very few (older ones) at the top. Obviously, the grandparents couldn't be living in the same house as *all* of their children's children if there were three or four different houses with grandchildren.

Moreover, there were simply far fewer grandparents around. In 1850, only 2 percent of the population lived past sixty-five. By 1900, the average life span had climbed to just forty-eight years for women and forty-six years for men. Given these limited life expectancies, most grandparents' lives did not overlap with their grandchildren's for a significant time period. A child born in 1900 had a better than 90 percent chance that two or more of his grandparents would be alive. But by the time he reached age fifteen, the chances were only about 50 percent that two or more grandparents would still be alive. Even if a grandchild and grandparent did live in the same house, the chances are that this was a brief phase, after which the household returned to its two-generation form.

The multigenerational families that have become part of modern folklore rarely existed in the past. In the late nineteenth and early twentieth century, less than 20 percent of urban American households contained relatives other than members of the nuclear family. (And not all of these relatives were grandparents.) According to historian Peter Laslett, the nuclear family has been the standard form of residence in England since the late sixteenth century!

To be sure, older persons were more likely to be living with their adult children then as opposed to today. But there just weren't very many of them, and if at all possible they lived with an unmarried child, usually a daughter. These caretaking spinsters paid a heavy price, sacrificing their personal happiness and chance to marry and raise a family for the sake of their parents.

In the past, elderly Americans sought, as they do today, to maintain their autonomy. Even in the nineteenth century, single-generation homes were the ideal. Older people, particularly widows, would often take in unrelated boarders to maintain their independence without slipping into poverty. It was mainly widows unable to maintain their own households who moved in with their married children or invited them into their houses.

Even in China and Japan, where cultural norms dictated coresidence of two adult generations, high mortality rates in the past limited the number of three-generation households. During most of Chinese history, the average household fluctuated between five and six residents, with a large proportion of nuclear families.

As fond as my memories are of the apartment I shared with my grandmother and parents in Frankfurt, I was left with few illusions that a three-generation household is an ideal situation. My mother and grandmother never really got along (a not-uncommon daughter-in-law and mother-in-law situation). I also remember that it was rather crowded. I slept in an alcove in my parents' room, and my grandmother's bedroom was also our living room.

Are We Moving Apart?

If grandparents didn't necessarily live in the same household, they must have lived close by. After all, didn't grandparents live, in the words of the song, "over the river and through the woods"? Our intuition says that as migration rates have increased, the elderly, including grandparents, find themselves farther and farther away from their children, grandchildren, and other relatives.

Recent research presents a very different picture, however. Peter Uhlenberg, one of the United States' leading demographers and experts on population patterns, has argued that there are numerous problems with the popular perception that families have drifted apart in recent years. First, he notes that census data do not indicate an increase in the tendency of native-born Americans to move outside their state of birth during the twentieth century. Indeed, at ages in which adults are most likely to have older parents (ages twenty-five to fifty-nine), the percentage living outside their state of birth appears to be lower than in 1910.

Of course, in-state can be hundreds of miles away, and it could be the grandparents who have moved, not the children. Look at all the people who have moved to Florida or Arizona! But more specific data only strengthens Uhlenberg's argument. According to the National Survey of Families and Household conducted in 1987-88, 74 percent of the elderly who had any adult children had at least one of them living within a twenty-five mile radius. This figure is almost identical to that found in surveys conducted a quarter of a century earlier, which found that 40 percent of adult children met with their parents at least once a week! In 1990 data from the American Association of Retired Persons, over half of adult children lived within a one-hour drive of their parents. There appears to be little reason, therefore, to accept descriptions of the elderly that depict them as living in isolation because they are so far away from kith and kin.

Although studies indicate that geographic proximity is a

major factor in determining how often family members speak to each other, either face-to-face or on the phone, *proximity generally has been found to have little or no impact on the level of emotional closeness or affect across generations.* In other words, being close (emotionally) is not just a matter of being nearby. Changing transportation and communications technologies have also reduced the significance of distance for relationships.

Too Close for Comfort?

Although most of the questions I get and complaints I hear come from grandparents who feel they are too far away from their grandchildren, I do need to say a few words about those cases in which distance, or actually the lack of distance, is an issue. As I have already indicated, most grandparents and parents prefer to live on their own and preserve their autonomy and independence. These days, sharing a house is usually the result of some sort of crisis—illness, death, or divorce—rather than a matter of preference. Even among Asian-Americans the trend seems to be away from three-generation households.

However, lots of grandparents live close by, either in the same building, on the same block, or in the same neighborhood. This raises its own issues and calls for special sensitivity.

How close is too close is less a matter of distance than a matter of style and mutual preference. It is possible to crowd your children when you live an hour away or to give them plenty of space when they live around the corner. From my own experience, when you live nearby, you need to be very careful to respect the parents' and grandchildren's right to live their own lives and make it clear to them that you want to live yours. Although it's wonderful to have the chance to be involved on such an immediate level, you need to be especially careful to respect their boundaries.

Take the question of visits. In the next chapter, I'll have much more to say about visits that are special trips planned in advance. Here I want to say a few words about the daily routine of visits, which don't require a lot of advance preparation. This is my own situation, since all of my grandchildren live in New York City and are rarely more than a cab ride away.

What I have learned is that it's a good idea to agree upon a visiting policy that works for both parents and grandparents. Given my busy schedule, I don't think my kids would ever think of just dropping by because they happened to be in the neighborhood. They know that except for weekends, I'm rarely home. But even if I were more of a homebody, I don't think I would appreciate being surprised just as I was about to go out, take a nap, or sit down for a good talk with an old friend. If that's the way you feel about things, be sure you let your children know.

But visits are a two-way street. Although you might want to drop in to see your granddaughter whenever the mood strikes you, this isn't a very good idea unless her parents have made it clear that they welcome such spontaneous visits. First of all, she may be asleep or out visiting a friend. In either of these cases, her parents may have been looking forward to some quiet time together, *alone*! And if you show up to see her just before mealtime or bedtime, you may prove to be an unappreciated distraction.

Another topic that requires special thought and consideration for nearby grandparents is baby-sitting. Although it is probably flattering to know that you are always the first choice when your children need a baby sitter (and not just because you don't charge!), being a grandparent doesn't mean that you have to give up your social life for their sake. Saying no doesn't mean you're a bad grandparent! Let your children know what they can expect from you in terms of baby-sitting: how often, which days of the week are best, and any other conditions you have.

One of my rules is that I don't baby-sit when what they need is someone to sit in the house while the children sleep. I view baby-sitting as a chance to spend time with my grandchildren, not an opportunity to catch up with my reading or television watching.

Holidays, birthdays, and other celebrations all call for special attention when you live nearby. The key here, as so often, is never to assume. (As the saying goes, when you assume, you make an *ass* out of *u* and *me*.) As much as you may want to be there always, to share every holiday and attend every birthday party, it's all too easy for these expectations to turn into a burden for both sides. Even if your children enjoy the tradition of such get-togethers, they may seem much less attractive to your grandchildren as they get older. Never take it for granted that you are invited or that they are coming to celebrate with you. Ask well in advance what their plans are, and if you are not part of them, accept it as graciously as possible.

The Loneliness of the Long-Distance Grandparent

Many grandparents I know would love to deal with the nearness issues I've just discussed. Even if some of your grandchildren live near enough for you to see them regularly, if you have several children, the chances that one or more of them and some of your grandchildren live far away increase. And the statistics I cited notwithstanding, there is little reassurance in knowing what the general situation is when your *own* grandchild is far away. So what do you do if your grandchildren are far away? Steve's mother has four grandchildren: a grandson and granddaughter in Israel and two granddaughters in Virginia. About a year ago, she left Pittsburgh, where she had lived for almost thirty years, and moved to Virginia, twenty minutes from her granddaughters. It hasn't solved the problem of the grandchildren in Israel, but it is a start. "I get to be a *real* grandmother," she says. She baby-sits, takes her granddaughters to swimming lessons, and sees them several times a week.

This kind of arrangement is most definitely not for everyone. It presupposes a level of harmony between parents and children and daughters- and sons-in-law. You may just be exchanging one set of issues for another. Many grandparents have jobs, friends, or other attachments that would keep them from making such a change. And not everyone would be able to afford such a move. But in cases where it could work, it is a wonderful solution to the problem of distance.

Assuming that you have no immediate plans to move closer to your grandchildren, there are many ways you can stay in touch when you're too far away to meet face to face.

Keep Yourself Up-to-Date

Whether you plan to call, write, e-mail, or fax, communication will always be easier if you are up-to-date with your grandchildren's interests. If you live nearby, this should take place quite naturally as part of your regular routine of visits and talks, but if you are far away, it takes more of an effort.

Do you know the name of your granddaughter's best friend? What about your grandson's favorite television show? I'm not suggesting that you quit your job so you can stay at home and watch "Barney and Friends," or the "Mighty Morphin Power Rangers," but you might want to join one of your friends the next time she takes her children or grandchildren to see the latest Disney film. Bob Kasey, founder of Creative Grandparenting Inc. in Wilmington, Delaware, has six grandchildren (five girls and one boy) who live in three different states. He keeps in practice as a grandparent by working in his organization's mentoring program, which pairs seniors with youths in ten of Delaware's elementary schools. Anything you can do that deepens your understanding of and experience with children your grandchildren's age can only help your relationships.

Remember that children grow up quickly, and when it comes to their interests, nothing is as *out* as last year's *in*. Before you go out and buy a Ninja Turtle knapsack or a Bart Simpson lunchbox, check that this is still what they want.

If your grandchild is very interested in a particular sport or athlete, it's well worth the effort of a few minutes to scan the sports page. Many preteen boys (and some teenage girls) go through a phase in which batting averages, three-point shots, interceptions, and goals (depending on which sport is being played) are the only thing that interests them. If your grandson is one of them, perhaps it should interest you as well. Find out what your grandchildren are reading (contrary to popular rumor, many children still do read books!) and read or reread it yourself.

Once they get a little older, you do not necessarily need to focus only on *their* interests. You can also begin to explore things that you can share. Some of the finest literature on the market today is being written for teens and young adults. Find a book that you think might interest your granddaughter. Send her a copy and keep one to read yourself. There are several books and online services that recommend such works, but I've usually found that my local bookstore is helpful enough. I have yet to read a Newberry Award winner (given by the American Library Association for the most distinguished contribution to American literature for children) or a Golden Kite-winning book (by the society of Children's Book Writers and Illustrators) that wasn't a great read. After you've both read the book, you can discuss it. For more about books and gifts, see Chapter 8.

Letter Writing

In the book for grandchildren that I wrote with Pierre Lehu, we devoted a lot of attention to the value of letter writing. In this age of telephones, faxes, and e-mail, letter writing is an all but forgotten practice. Most young children have never done it, and even when we don't talk to our friends on the phone it rarely occurs to us to write. When was the last time you received a nice long, juicy letter? Having grandchildren is an excellent opportunity to revive an old custom.

One of the most important things to remember about letters is that they are both a form of communication for the present and a record for the future. Ask your grandchildren to keep a copy of your letters, but to be on the safe side, keep a copy yourself.

When I was sent to Switzerland to save me from the Nazis, my parents and grandmother wrote me on a regular basis for as long as they could. Although they knew that the Nazis would read their letters (and my replies) and thus had to be careful, they tried to keep in touch with me as much as possible by sending me poems and birthday greetings and as much news as the censors would allow.

My grandmother would often send me grandmotherly advice, as in the letter she wrote on April 10, 1941:

> Thank God you are well taken care of, and the sky and the sun are over us here as everywhere, just as rains and storms are everywhere. Enjoy your carefree youth and gather strength for the serious life ahead. Stay healthy and happy. All your relatives send their best wishes for happy holidays. With all my best wishes for you, I am your loving grandma.

I still have all the letters they sent, and I treasure them dearly, even though they are more than fifty years old. I only wish that they contained more details. But there are no censors looking over your shoulder when you write, so include as much information as you can. Even if your grandchildren don't appreciate the letters now, they probably will in the future. Letter writing is only one way of fulfilling your role of family historian, as discussed in Chapter 5.

Don't limit yourself to writing standard letters. Even your youngest grandchildren can look at pictures and, if you have the skill, drawings that you send. As they get a little older, you can send them picture letters, in which the message is conveyed by a few pictures or drawings (for example, a picture of a deer and one of your grandson equals "Dear grandson").

If there's a cartoon or comic strip you think your granddaughter would appreciate, send it to her. And as she gets older, you can send interesting newspaper articles or clippings about her favorite actor, basketball player, or movie star. Send a disposable camera with an addressed and stamped mailing envelope, and ask your grandchild to take pictures and send them to you. And don't forget to send pictures and postcards when you travel!

Once children get used to the idea that there may be letters arriving containing news, pictures, stories, and other treats *intended especially for them*, they will come to look forward to them. Despite all our technological advances, most people I know feel a little rush of anticipation when they open their mail and hidden in among the bills, solicitations, and magazines is a personal letter.

You're Only a Phone Call Away

Twentieth-century technology has vastly changed our ability to communicate over distance. Although it hardly seems believable today, at the end of World War II only half of American homes had a telephone. Even in the late 1950s as many as a quarter of households had no telephone. (Our grandchildren will probably find it just as hard to imagine that in 1990 only 27 percent of U.S. households had a home computer!)

Today, of course, the telephone is part of the old technology, and only a handful of families—such as the Amish, who have chosen to do without—don't have phones. If you're from the generation that can still remember when there was one phone company and no one was competing to get your business, the phone may still seem impersonal to you. No one can say that I'm not a big fan of telephones; I spend hours on the phone every day. But long-distance grandparenting over the phone is not something I'm very fond of. The youngest grandchildren can't even talk. Even the older ones may turn monosyllabic and answer every question with "Yes," "No," "Fine," or "OK." On the other hand, if the conversation takes off, it can cost a lot of money. I certainly wouldn't make the phone the only link between you and your grandchildren, but it's good for them to hear your voice on a regular basis.

There are a number of things you can do to make the most of your phone calls. First and foremost. work on your timing. Find out when the best times are to call your grandchildren. Although evenings may be best as far as rates are concerned, just before bedtime may *not* be very good for parents of small children. An exciting call from grandpa just before they're supposed to go to sleep may not be appreciated. Ask your children what times are convenient for them.

With older grandchildren, particularly those living at home, you may have other restrictions. High school or college-age grandchildren may appreciate the break from homework or studying for tests, so long as you don't call when they're feeling particularly pressured.

Although it's good to be spontaneous and call "just for the hell of it," timing your calls with special events can also help the conversation along and give everyone a feeling of your personal involvement. This is true not only for the obvious, such as birthday greetings, but also before an important game or school play and after report cards come out or a big party takes place.

Remember that no matter how young your grandchildren are, they can still listen and learn to recognize your voice. Somewhat older children may enjoy it when you call just to talk to them. You may want to encourage your high school–age grandchildren to call you collect or use your calling card.

(Be sure you make it clear that this is not an invitation to charge all their calls to you!)

Audio Letters

Before we get into some of the really new ways of communicating with your grandchildren, let me say a few words about a very simple method that is a departure from either letters or phone calls: audio tapes. All you need is a cassette tape recorder and a blank tape, and you're ready to roll.

The easiest thing to do is just talk into the tape recorder and send the tape as a "letter." This is especially helpful if your grandchildren are too young to read a written letter. Not only do they get your message, but they hear your voice without the pressure of a long-distance phone call.

You may want to leave one side of the tape blank so that your children and grandchildren can fill it up and send it back to you. You can then record over it, but personally I like the idea of saving it for posterity. Years from now your grandchildren not only will be able to hear your words but will hear your voice saying them!

Although sending an audio letter may be the easiest thing to do, there is no reason why you shouldn't be more creative. If there's a book your grandson particularly likes you can record it on tape and he can listen to you reading it to him. Lots of toy stores sell books with cassettes in which the child looks at the book while listening to a tape, which makes a distinctive noise or tells him to turn the page. I have always thought that armed with a tape recorder and tapes, any grandparent could make her own copies of such book-tape sets. If you are more comfortable just reading the words in the book that's fine, but you might want to tell the story to your grandchild by adding personal asides to make it more intimate. Going a step further, you can make up stories of your own, sing songs, or recite nursery rhymes.

If some of your grandchildren are nearby and others farther away, you might want to try and organize a cousins' tape or make a recording of a family event such as a birthday party or holiday celebration.

And of course, you can also encourage your faraway grandchildren to make tapes and send them to you. This can be especially nice if your granddaughter plays an instrument, sings in a choir, or is in a play. If there's a song she especially likes, she can send you a copy on tape (much cheaper than buying you a copy of an entire cassette or CD album), although be prepared if you get something rather loud by a group you've never heard of!

Lights, Cameras, Action!

Moving up the technology scale, you can also use video to send messages to your grandchildren. Here again, you should explore the whole range of options. You can set up the camera and film yourself talking, but personally I don't think this is all that interesting. With the help of a friend, you can film yourself doing all sorts of daily activities, such as working, baking, or playing sports. Family events are a natural for videotaping, as are trips of any length.

It is even more fun to *receive* tapes of your children and grandchildren. If your children are like lots of parents I know, the hard thing isn't going to be convincing them to video their kids, but to stop long enough to send you a copy of the tapes.

Video cameras have become so popular that at many school plays there are so many cameras in evidence and parents jostling to get the best angles that they look like *paparazzi* jostling for a shot of Tom Cruise or Demi Moore.

The Fax of Life

Although computers are probably the most talked about advance in communications technology, they are only one alternative to such traditional methods of communication as the letter and the phone. Fax (facsimile) machines are comparatively cheap and easy to operate, and although you probably associate them with office equipment, more and more people have them in their homes.

The biggest advantage of the fax over regular mail is that it allows you to instantly send or receive a letter, newspaper clipping, report card, or other message. You don't have to worry about sticking something in an envelope and mailing it. Since the original stays with you, you can send a letter to your grandchild *and* keep the original. (Who says you can't have your cake and eat it too?)

Since you only pay for the time on the line, which is usually brief, it's cheaper than a phone call and *you don't have to worry about catching people at home or timing your call for the right time.*

I think a fax machine for the home is a wonderful gift idea for the grandparents, especially if the children or grandchildren already have one.

Computers

Although I have a website and there's a CD-ROM version of my book *Dr. Ruth's Encyclopedia of Sex*, I have to admit I'm a computer illiterate. I don't even know how to turn on a computer, much less work on one.

I know I'm not alone. Plenty of people in their forties and fifties not to mention their sixties don't feel comfortable with computers. They feel they're too old to be taking courses and find big computer books intimidating. Who doesn't feel a little inadequate watching some teenage computer whiz playing games and surfing the web? At times it seems that computer programs and games are intentionally made "adult-proof."

First of all, it's important to stress that many seniors have learned to use and enjoy computers. Twenty percent of people sixty-five to sixty-nine years old own a computer. So if you're like me and you are not very good at typing and think a mousepad is a cage for small rodents, do not let that fool you into thinking that you can't become computer literate.

So what, I hear you say. You've lived your whole life without using a computer. Why start now? I'm not going to try and sell you on computers by listing all the marvelous things you can do with them. I'll mention only two: communication and information.

One of the easiest things to do with a computer is correspond by e-mail. It's not only easy but comparatively inexpensive. Just imagine being able to chat back and forth with your grandchildren who live across the country for the price of a local phone call. Moreover, with e-mail you don't have to worry if it is a good time to call (write). Your message will be waiting for them whenever they go on-line. Lots of kids have gotten so used to communicating on-line that it's their favorite medium. Not only will your computer give you a new means of communication with your grandchildren, it also can provide a new shared topic of communication. Many of our grandchildren are remarkably adept with computers and delight in solving our problems or offering advice on how to get the most out of your computer.

Computers are also a means to access vast amounts of useful information without leaving your house. Suppose you want to know about custody issues or recent books about grandparenting like this one. Maybe you want to chat with other grandparents who are raising their grandchildren or get some gift-giving advice. When I was at my publishers' offices to discuss this book, they found 546 items on grandparenting, offering advice, resources, chat groups, and legal information. I have only been able to include a few of these at various points in this book. Computers really do give us the world at our fingertips. Why should they be wasted on the young?

It's All a Matter of Timing

Yet another way to share experiences with your grandchildren who are far away is to work on your timing. Even when you can't be together in terms of geography, you can synchronize your schedules to bring you closer together. You can arrange to watch a certain television show or movie at the same time or at least within a day of each other and then discuss it or exchange letters. Similarly, you can rent the same video of a recent film or one of your old favorites and then use it as the basis for conversation.

Another way to erase the miles is to coordinate your celebrations. Light birthday candles at the same time regardless of where you are, or open presents under your tree regardless of when Christmas morning comes in your part of the world.

Then share the experience by calling, faxing, or e-mailing your loved ones.

Traveling Together

Even if you don't live near your grandchildren, you can share time together in different ways. The most obvious, of course, is for them to visit you, either with or without their parents, or for you to visit them. (I'll have more to say on both these options in the next chapter.) But another thing that can be lots of fun is going on a trip with your grandchildren.

The best age to travel with most grandchildren is probably when they are between six and eleven. They are old enough to be fun and not require constant supervision, independent enough to spend the time away from their parents, and young enough not to feel that anything that doesn't involve their friends is an embarrassment or a waste of time.

If you want to make such a trip, be sure to involve your grandchild as much as possible in the planning, so that you can anticipate what will make the trip a good experience for her. Also share with her your ideas for the trip, particularly what your expectations are in terms of behavior. Make sure that the parents have made it clear to the child that *you* are in charge for the duration of the trip.

Grandparents who would like to arrange a trip with a grandchild can also contact Grandtravel, a Maryland travel agency that will arrange intergenerational trips to the American Southwest, the Australian Outback, or pretty much anywhere in between. They print a set of firm guidelines for behavior, such as being quiet in public places, no playing on elevators, and no littering. They can be reached at:

Grandtravel
6900 Wisconsin Avenue
Suite 706
Chevy Chase, MD 20815
1-800-288-5575

Another option is:

R.F.D. Travel Corporation,
"Grandparents & Grandchildren"
Contact: Mary Beatty
5201 Johnson Drive
Shawnee Mission, KS 66205
1-800-365-5359

Arthur and Carol Kornhaber of the Foundation for Grandparenting hold a grandparent/grandchild camp every summer in New York's Adirondack Mountains. You can contact them at:

Grandparents' and Grandchildren's Camp
Sagamore
P.O. Box 146
Raquette Lake, NY 13436
315-354-5311

Further Reading

FRY, PATRICIA L. *Creative Grandparenting Across the Miles* (Liquori Publications, 1997).

KERR, GWENYTH. *Grandparenting Long Distance: 35 Easy Ways to Stay in Touch & Keep the Love Alive* (Sunrise Publications, 1996).

KOFTAN, KENNETH and JENELLE. *Long-Distance Grandparenting: Books 1-3* (Spring Creek Pubns, 1988). Three volumes discussing issues for different ages.

WASSERMAN, SELMA. *The Long-Distance Grandmother: How to Stay Close to Distant Children*, 3rd. ed. (Vancouver, B.C.: Hartley & Marks, 1996).

Too Faraway Grandparents Newsletter
Mike Moldovan
P.O. Box 71
Del Mar, CA 92014
Write for a sample issue.

7

It Pays to Visit!

The most exciting experience for the long-distance grandparent is when you go to visit your grandchildren or they come to visit you. For a brief time, whether it is a few days or a week or two, you get to spend real time together, eating, playing, and going places.

As any grandparent can testify, there is a world of difference between going to visit your grandchildren and having them come to spend time at your house. For most of us, being the guest is so much less complicated. Playing host to your grandchildren is usually a much greater challenge, which I will discuss in some detail in the second part of this chapter.

Grandma's Coming!

If all your grandchildren live close by and most of your visits don't last more than a few hours, most of what I have to say here will not be immediately relevant. Hopefully, your visits to them will be frequent, and you and your children will have worked out a routine that suits everyone. Many parents I know have a rule of no unannounced visits, but you can work out your own ground rules about visits from nearby grandparents.

If you live far away and come less often but stay longer, each visit becomes an event. We all know the scenario: Everyone has been planning and talking about the big visit. You arrive tired from the drive, train ride, or flight. The youngest grandchild doesn't quite remember you. Your daughter-in-law feels like she's under a microscope. It feels like the coming week is going to last an eternity.

Probably the two most important decisions regarding any visit are when to come and how long to stay. Holidays are, of course, a wonderful time to get together. My husband Fred's parent's lived in Europe in the days when phone calls were more expensive, air travel less common, and e-mail and faxes were the stuff of science fiction. It was very important to all of us that they would visit us in New York every year for Passover.

Holidays offer a unique opportunity to pass down family traditions and share special moments. They are also the time when *most* people want to be with family, so don't make an issue of it if your children decide to invite the other side of the family or travel to visit other relatives themselves. Holidays also often carry with them an enormous emotional burden. Everyone seems to have memories of a particularly wonderful Thanksgiving, Christmas, or Easter, and somehow it never seems to be *this* one. As the family grows through marriage and the birth of children, traditional arrangements seem to get harder and harder to preserve. Holidays and other special occasions are also when relatives who are absent because of divorce, death, or distance are most missed.

Since you are the guest it is a good idea to be as flexible as possible regarding the timing of your visit. When discussing a visit with your children, it is best to have several different dates in mind. Of course, if you are working, it will depend to a large extent on when you can get vacation time.

If your children are like most young couples with children, there is rarely such thing as an ideal time for a visit. Get a clear idea of what their schedule is like before making your final plans. For example, if your daughter's business has a busy season, she may prefer you not come at that time because things will be too hectic. On the other hand, she may want you to come when her work is particularly demanding precisely because it will make child care a little easier.

You need to be clear on what kind of role you want to play during the visit. If you are willing to watch the children after school, cook, or go on day trips, so much the better, but if you've come to relax and play, be sure you and your children don't get your signals crossed.

In trying to decide how long to visit, it is helpful to remember the old adage: fish and relatives start to smell after three days. So a long weekend is probably an ideal length of time. If your children live across the country, a long weekend can seem very short. The longer your travel time, the longer you will probably make your visit. And the longer your visit, the trickier it gets.

All things being equal, you probably would like to stay with your children and grandchildren. This is cheaper than any alternative and certainly gives more of a feeling of family. But if your children live in a small place, they may not have room. You may find sleeping on the couch rather trying after a week. If there is a guest room, you can stay longer without disrupting everyone's routine.

Renting a room in a nearby hotel or motel may cost some money, but it also provides somewhere to go to rest, have a quiet cup of coffee, and escape whenever everyone needs a time-out. Fred and I were fortunate. His parents were well-off. They stayed in a hotel when they visited us in New York. We also visited them every summer in Switzerland, where they put us up in a hotel. We did visit them once at home in Portugal, but we all found it better to meet on neutral territory, traveling to a vacation spot and staying there.

To Grandfather's House We Go

By the time the youngest children have learned to keep the house tidy, the oldest grandchildren are on hand to tear it to pieces.

Christopher Morley

Again, if your grandchildren live nearby and most of their visits don't last more than a few hours some of what I have to say next will not be immediately relevant. Yes, you still need to childproof your house and deal with house rules, but it is a far more gradual and less intensive process. If they live far away and come less often but stay longer, each visit becomes an event.

We all know the scenario, it is your visit in reverse. Everyone has been planning and talking about the big visit to the grandparents for days or even weeks. The children and grandchildren arrive tired from the ride or flight. The youngest doesn't want to sleep in a strange bed. The oldest complains that there's nothing to do. Your daughter-in-law feels like she is under a microscope. After an hour you're exhausted from getting everyone settled and worrying that your three-year-old granddaughter is either going to break something or hurt herself, or both. It feels like the coming week is going to last an eternity.

No matter how much you love your grandchildren and look forward to being with them, having them in your house can be quite a strain. It is *your* house and if all your own children are grown and have moved out, you've probably gotten used to a routine. Whether that means going from activity to activity all day long or sitting at home and reading or watching television, it's what makes you comfortable. Your house is set up the way you like it. Having any houseguests for an extended period can be disruptive. When houseguests are much younger and much louder, it can really throw you for a loop.

Be Realistic

Be realistic about your abilities to play host. Do you have enough room? Is there somewhere for the children to play? Are small children welcome in your building? Are you physically up to it? Before you decide that a trip to a particular theme park or sports complex will be part of the visit, ask around to make sure that others won't find it too exhausting.

Nothing can get a visit off on the wrong foot as quickly as unrealistic expectations. The more people involved, the more likely things are to get complicated. Children often get sick when traveling. Planes arrive late, and snow and rain usually fall when it's least convenient. If you expect everything to be perfect and you see it as a crisis each time things don't go as planned, it's very hard to really enjoy a visit. Remember that your relationship with your grandchildren and adult children is the product of years of investment and work, not of any one visit. As the saying goes, "If you want God to laugh, make plans."

One friend of mine always stays with a high school friend when he brings the grandchildren to visit his parents. Not only does his friend have more room, he also has toys, games, a yard, and children more or less the same age. You may want to consider renting a room in a nearby hotel or motel for your guests if you or they can afford it.

Remember that your routine will be disrupted. Do not expect to do everything you normally do on top of playing host. Take time off from work or at least try to cut back your hours. Keep your social calendar as clear as possible; your friends will understand. Try to tie up loose ends in advance, but don't run yourself into exhaustion before the visit even begins.

If you and your adult children have trouble getting along for a few hours at a time, spending a week together in the same house may not be a good idea until things have improved. Read Chapter 2, "Common Concerns," again. Even if you stay together, it doesn't mean that you all need to be together 24-7 (twenty-four hours a day, seven days a week). It is a good idea to plan for some rest time for all the adults, including yourself. In addition, you will probably want to have some time with each of your grandchildren alone and with each of the parents as well.

If you feel that your children are too lenient with their children, this is not the time to show everyone how it should be done. Of course, there have to be certain house rules. Discuss these in advance with the parents; don't spring them on everyone out of the blue. Consider your priorities. As always, safety comes first. Be firm about keeping your grandchildren out of harm's way. In general, house rules should be about the house, not about dictating everyone's daily routine. No smoking indoors, no food in the living room, no climbing on the furniture, and no outdoor games (like catch) inside the house all certainly fall within the former category. But rules such as no television before supper or no dessert unless you finish all the food on your plate are just going to create tensions unless that's the way it is when the grandchildren are at home.

If you really enjoy spoiling your grandchildren, remember that when they come on a longer visit they need discipline and routine as well. As much as you may enjoy playing with your grandchildren, when their parents say it's bedtime, accept their decision. And if the kids protest, keep your peace.

Once you have lowered your expectations, the three most important things you can do to have a successful visit are *prepare, prepare, prepare.*

Childproof Your House

There are companies these days that will come to your house and tell you how to childproof it. They will tell you what to put away and even install everything necessary, like childproof cabinet latches. To me that seems to be going a bit overboard, but don't underestimate the importance of properly preparing your house for young guests. If you have other grandchildren who live nearby, you may have already done this. But remember that every age is different. Ask friends who have children or grandchildren the same age to come by (without the children!) and give you advice.

Here are a few key reminders:

1. Add the Poison Control number to your usual list of emergency numbers posted near your phone.

2. Get on the floor to check for small items—coins, nuts, buttons—that might cause choking.

3. Secure drapery or blind pulls out of reach, and be sure that any windows low enough to be opened by a child have a safety latch.

4. Put plastic safety covers on all unused electrical outlets.

5. Keep potentially poisonous houseplants out of reach, and be sure that your grandchildren are well supervised if you take them to play in your garden or yard.

6. Set your water heater at 120°F to prevent accidental scalding. If you have boiling water on tap, shut it off during their visit.

7. Put a nonskid mat in the bathtub.

8. Never leave a child in or near standing water. In the time it takes for you to get a towel or answer the phone, a child can slip under the water. Drain the tub immediately after you've finished using it.

9. Use childproof caps on all medications and vitamin and mineral supplements. (Your pharmacist can give you replacements.)

10. Be sure that matches or cigarette lighters are where your grandchildren cannot get to them. Put household chemicals, including all cleaning supplies, out of reach, not under the sink. Remember, where young children are concerned, plastic bags are hazardous objects.

11. Keep tables and countertops free of knives, scissors, appliance cords, and piles of heavy objects, such as books, that can easily tip over. Children can reach higher than you think.

12. Cook on the back burners, turning pot handles toward the middle of the stove.

13. Make sure that any doors you don't want opened have a latch. This includes kitchen, bathroom, and liquor cabinets; doors leading to the cellar or garage; and gates at the top and bottom of stairs. Remember, even a couple of stairs can be a danger to a small child. Be sure, also, that any doors that have inside locks or latches can be opened from the outside as well. (Nothing disrupts a day like a small child locking himself into the bathroom.) Telling children that a particular place, such as your bedroom or the basement, is off limits may make it only more mysterious. You have every right to expect them to respect your wishes, but don't rely on the fact that you *told* them to stay out to keep them out of danger.

14. Never leave a cat or dog unattended with a young child. Even the most gentle of animals will react if he is teased and poked enough. Be sure that birds, fish, and other pets are out of reach.

15. Be sure that all guns and firearms are locked away. Bullets and the keys to the gun locker should be locked away separately.

16. Make sure you have children's aspirin, a thermometer, Band-aids, and the name of a good pediatrician.

Find Out What Your Guests Need

Traveling with children means striking a fine balance between the new and the familiar. Chances are, especially with younger children, that they will be excited enough at the beginning. So don't overwhelm them with presents, new games, or things to do the minute they arrive. Once things have calmed down, you can liven them up with surprises and gifts.

If your children have come by plane, they have probably had to think carefully about what they could bring and what they had to leave behind. One way you can be a big help is by having a ready supply of nonessentials on hand at your house. A good supply of books, games, stuffed animals, and the like, are a good starting point. If you don't already have the books, you may want to borrow some from friends (be sure to write down what you take, so you can separate them from your own stuff at the end of the visit) or your local library. When you're at the library, you might check out their video collection, although you can also rent from your local video store.

Although you want to be sure to have basics available when everyone arrives, don't feel that you have to have a week's supply of activities in the house on the first day. A trip to the library, toy store, or local video shop can make for a pleasant outing, and your chances of making the right choice go way up if your grandchildren are with you.

At the same time as you ask about toys and other fun things, ask the parents about their practical needs for the trip: diapers, wipes, a high chair, car seat, and so forth. They'll bring many of these things with them, and some you or they can certainly buy, but it's hardly the first thing that anyone wants to think about right after arriving. So find out what they'll need, and then rent or borrow a crib, high chair, or car seat. The last of these is especially important. If your family is arriving by plane and you are picking them up at the airport, you'll need to have a child seat (or seats) already in your car when they arrive. Even if they are coming by car, you may want to install a child seat in your car to avoid switching of cars and limits on your maneuverability if only their car is child-equipped.

Food for Thought

If your family is like a lot of families I know, much of the day seems to be taken up with food preparation, eating, and cleaning up (or making reservations, traveling, ordering, eating, going home). In any event, meals and snacks will probably make up a big part of your grandchildren's visit.

What do they like to eat? Small children can be incredibly fussy. You may know that pale yellow cheddar cheese tastes the same as orange cheddar cheese, but do you want to have a fight over it? Meals will probably be chaotic enough without extra problems. We've all been told that breakfast is the most important meal of the day. It's certainly one of the most important ones to plan for. So don't get your day off on the wrong foot by not having a child's favorite breakfast cereal. Ask the parents about other food preferences and needs. Fast food, pizza, and sweets can be a wonderful treat, but not as their regular diet for an entire week.

It is a good idea to discuss your children's rules about snacks before they arrive. As our understanding of nutrition has grown, more and more parents have decided to limit their kids' intake of sugar, salt, and oily foods. There is no point in stocking up on all sorts of sweets and goodies if most of the things you buy are on the parents' "forbidden" list. Even if your children are fairly easygoing about such matters, you should plan to have a ready supply of healthier items like fruits, yogurts, and juices.

When do they usually eat? If you are the sort of person who

loves routine and believes that supper should be on the table at exactly the same time every day, family visits can be a bit of a shock. For practical reasons (bath times, homework, and early bedtimes) many families with small children eat rather early. This doesn't mean you have to change your schedule, but be prepared to make adjustments. If you expect your grandchildren to eat at a later time, you may have to prepare some sort of snack to tide them over.

For some people I know, the kitchen is their special place. It would never occur to them to have someone else putter around in there, much less prepare a meal. Of course, if you don't like having other people in your kitchen, you can't complain if you have to do all the cooking! At best it can be rather tiring when you're preparing food for additional mouths. What is even worse is that much of the time you could be sharing with your grandchildren is spent in another room, preparing for or cleaning up from a meal.

If your grandchildren are really young, someone will have to keep them busy while the meals are being prepared. If your grandchildren are a bit older, then it is much easier to turn meal preparation into a shared family experience. This is a wonderful opportunity to share family recipes or little hints about how you make a special dish. Put your grandson to work helping to make dinner. (Be sure that younger children are kept away from sharp knives or other potentially dangerous utensils.) Even if you don't prepare a whole meal together, baking a cake or a batch of cookies can be lots of fun.

Going out to eat with the whole family can also be fun if it's done intelligently. Contrary to popular belief, this does not mean limiting yourself to fast food joints or theme restaurants that are as much video arcades as eateries. It *does* mean checking in advance that the restaurant you've chosen welcomes children. This usually means having plenty of high chairs (it does no one any good if the restaurant only has two and they are both occupied when you arrive), children's menus, and some puzzles or other activities to keep the younger ones occupied while they wait for their food. For your part, it is important that you and the parents are very clear with your grandchildren about your expectations regarding behavior, such as waiting patiently for the food to be served and talking in a quiet "restaurant voice." If you are not sure whether a particular place is suitable for children your grandchildren's age, ask around. Don't just decide to try it out.

The Party Is Over

Be prepared for a letdown when they leave. After a week (or longer) of guests you may think that all you will want to do is sit at home and enjoy the quiet. By all means, get some rest, but beware of post-parting depression. Plan some activities that you particularly enjoy. Get together with your friends, especially the ones you haven't been able to spend time with while your family was visiting. Treat yourself to a movie, a nice dinner, or a play. Then start thinking about the next visit!

8

Giving Wisely

Better Off and More Able to Give

As we have already seen, grandparents today are younger and healthier and live longer than ever before. They are also far better off financially.

Amid all the debate that is going on today about the crisis in Social Security and health care, it is easy to forget what things were like before these programs existed. Almost without exception, the responsibility for aging family members fell to the younger family members. In the past, the big question was often which family member was going to be economically responsible for grandpa when he stopped working or for grandma after grandpa's death. Today, grandpa and grandma are more likely to be well provided for and asking themselves how they can help out their children and grandchildren.

Although it's nice to imagine an idyllic period when younger relatives cared for their elders without tension or resentment, neither historical nor cross-cultural studies support such a view. Although elderly people were accorded a higher social status in colonial times than they are today, they still lived in insecurity. In the words of family historian Tamar Hareven, "Aging parents had to enter into contracts with their inheriting sons in order to secure support in old age. . . . The emphasis in such contractual arrangements on specific details suggests the potential tensions and insecurities that parents anticipated concerning their care." In other words, elderly parents signed contracts because they were uncertain that their sons would meet their obligations and care for them in their old age.

Nor were older people in urban industrial America of the nineteenth and early twentieth century guaranteed support from their children. It is a testimony to how short our historical memories are that so few of us remember the poverty that was a routine part of old age less than fifty years ago. In the early 1950s, the income for most elderly households was near or below the poverty line. Even in the 1960s, 30 percent of elderly men and 40 percent of elderly women were poor. The noted Swedish sociologist Gunnar Myrdal, one of this century's most perceptive observers of twentieth-century American society, wrote of the "terrifying extent to which old people [in the United States] are left in poverty and destitution."

The changes since Myrdal penned these words could not have been more dramatic. By 1982, the elderly were no more likely to be poor than the rest of the population, and throughout the 1980s elderly households saw their income improve at a far faster rate than other households. These overall statistics somewhat mask the continued high rates of poverty found among widows and members of minority groups and do not do justice to the many elderly who live just above the poverty line. Nevertheless, there is little question that Social Security,

Medicare, widespread pension plans, and wiser investing have changed the economic character of relations across the generations. Grandparents are less likely to be financially dependent on their children for support. In fact, it is more common than ever for grandparents, both those who are still working and those who have retired, to provide financial assistance to the younger generations rather than the other way around.

Moreover, as the *Toy Trade News* (which has an obvious interest in the matter) recently reported, the proliferation of "bean-pole families" has had a dramatic effect on the "grand ratio" (the number of grandchildren under age ten per grandparent). In 1950 there were 2.4 such grandchildren for every grandparent. By the early 1990s it had dropped to 1.2 to 1, and by the year 2000 it is projected to be 1 to 1. What this means is not only will grandparents have more money, but they will have fewer grandchildren to spend it on. In other words, not only can we expect the $8.3 billion (!) grandparents spend on their grandchildren annually to grow in total, but each grandchild will be getting a bigger piece of the pie.

The Gift Relationship

Thus far in this book I have been discussing the different ways you can share your love and time with your grandchildren. I believe that we must never lose sight of the fact that these are the most precious things you have to give your grandchildren. You are in a unique position as a grandparent, and no one else can fill that role.

One of the most tangible ways in which you can express your feelings for your grandchildren is by giving them presents that convey your love, expand their horizons, ease their lives, and just simply bring them joy. As the French sociologist Marcel Mauss noted in his classic study, *The Gift*, gifts are not just materialistic exchanges. They are symbols of different types of relationships, and they build ties between people. On some level we all understand this principle and use it almost unconsciously when we search for a gift that is appropriate for a friend or relative (not too cheap, not too expensive, not too personal, or not too impersonal). So long as you view the presents you give your grandchildren not as a substitute for spending time with them nor as compensation for a lack of intimacy, but as an integral part of your overall relationship, you should be able to judge wisely when, what, and how much to give.

Informed Giving

The better you know your grandchildren and the more aware you are of their daily lives, the easier it will be for you to find just the right gift to give them. Spending time in their rooms, playing with them, and listening to their interests will all help you get the most bang for your buck. Ideally, giving a gift should be the beginning of a story, not its end. If the last time you see or hear of or talk about a gift you've given is when you give it, it's much less fulfilling than when it serves as the catalyst for a conversation or shared experience.

It is also a good idea to stay in close contact with your children regarding the gifts you plan to give to their children. On birthdays and holidays, this will help avoid duplication. And if you live far away, it will keep you up-to-date on current interests and wishes. This sort of consultation is absolutely vital for any gift that will require a major investment of time or energy on the part of the child or parents, such as a pet or a trip. (Be sure to avoid putting the parents on the spot: "I'd love to buy you a puppy. Go ask your father if that's OK.") It's also very important to be well informed about your children's house rules regarding violent toys and age-appropriate materials. Many of the videos and games on the market today are quite explicit when it comes to violence and adult language.

A Fairness Doctrine

If you have more than one grandchild, you are inevitably going to be concerned about being fair in your gift-giving. If you remember that the gifts you give are part of a relationship, not an end in themselves, this should be easier. Being fair does not mean giving the same thing to each of your grandchildren, giving a gift to each of them when you give something to one, or even spending precisely equal amounts on them. It means treating them as individuals and finding ways to give each one the gifts that will bring the most pleasure.

It is a good idea, however, to keep track of your gift-giving, especially if some of your grandchildren live close by and see you frequently and others are far away. One New York grandfather I know was surprised to discover that he was spending almost twice as much on his Connecticut granddaughter as on the one in Florida.

I know this may seem rather petty to you, but I have at least one friend who still harbors resentment over the favoritism her grandparents showed her brother. And your adult children may also resent it if they feel that their children are getting shortchanged in favor of their cousins.

While we are on the topic of competition, don't get yourself into the trap of competing with your in-laws as to which grandparents can spend the most money. It is hard to give wisely if you are thinking more about your in-laws than your grandchild. If you have less money, you just need to be a little more creative and original in your gift-giving and generous with what you do have, whether it be time or attention. Be happy that your grandchildren can benefit from the extras they receive from the other side of the family.

For All but the Youngest

The presents you give your grandchildren will depend on their ages, interests, and what their parents and others have bought for them already. As a rule, it's best to consult with either your children or grandchildren before buying, especially for very large or expensive gifts. Going into a toy store and asking for advice is usually an invitation to be offered the latest overpriced fad toy. Everyone has their favorite toys, books, and other gifts. Here are a few types of presents that I have found were well appreciated and can be suited to almost any age, except for babies and small infants.

It's My Bag

No matter what age your grandchildren are, they will need bags to carry things around with them. It may be a school bag if they are in elementary school or a backpack for those in their teens. The athlete in the family may need a sports bag for carrying equipment like rackets, uniforms, or bathing suits. A grandchild heading off to Europe or on a cross-country trip will probably appreciate a sturdy suitcase, a duffel bag, or a really good knapsack. All of the above come in varying sizes, shapes, styles, and colors. You many want to go shopping together to make just the right choice, or trust your instincts.

School Supplies

I know this doesn't sound very exciting. I can just hear it now: "Oh, grandma. Thank you for the lovely pencil case." There are actually many school-related gifts that will elicit a genuine smile. A lunch box, Thermos, or book bag with your grandchild's favorite cartoon figure or superhero usually are well received by elementary school age children. Diaries, calculators, and basic reference books such as dictionaries and thesauruses are usually appreciated by older students. A desk lamp, alarm clock, or small cassette recorder (for recording lectures) all make good presents for the college-bound grandchild.

If your resources are somewhat greater, you might buy your grandson in junior high a new desk or your college-bound granddaughter a laptop computer. (Paying for education itself is a very complex issue, and I'll have more to say on it later in this chapter.)

Wares to Wear

Although clothes are wonderful gifts, they are also, in my experience, among the riskiest. For the youngest children, they often end up being more of a gift to the parents. (Have you ever heard a child actually say he wanted warm socks and a scarf for his birthday?) This doesn't mean that you shouldn't give them. But don't expect that to be your most memorable present.

When buying clothes for younger children, think practical as well as pretty. Lots of buttons may look nice, but it may make the garment a nightmare to get on and take off. Remember that school clothes need to be sturdy enough for play as well as study. Take the parents into consideration as well. Stay-press and machine-wash may be more their style than things that need to be dry cleaned and ironed.

For older children, it is hard to keep up with the current styles, brand-names, and—when they are going through a growing spurt—sizes. Ask before you shop. If your grandchildren are willing to go shopping with you, you can pick things out together. If you know a store they particularly like, you can take your chances, and if worse comes to worst, they can take your gift in to exchange it. If all else fails, you might try a gift certificate.

Books and Magazines

Books are a lot like Mark Twain: Reports of their demise are greatly exaggerated. Everytime a new technological innovation comes along, the doomsayers report that kids are spending too much time in front of the television, computer, or video game and have stopped reading.

In fact, the most important influences on children's reading habits are their parents and those around them. Children who have grown up surrounded by readers and people who love books are much more likely to read *in addition to* enjoying all the other entertainments available today. Children's interest in reading begins long before they can read themselves; it starts by having people around who read to them.

The first books you get your grandchildren will probably be for them to look at and touch and for you to read. There is nothing quite like the feeling of opening a new book, sitting your grandchild on your lap, and reading the story. As they grow older, you can have the pleasure of introducing them to some of your own favorites from your childhood.

There are so many books out there that you may have a problem choosing which one to buy. *The New York Times Parent's Guide to the Best Books for Children*, by Edna Ross Lipton, (Random House, 1991) offers numerous valuable tips, even it doesn't have the absolute latest favorites. The big chain stores, which seem to be everywhere, usually have a huge selection of new children's books as well many of the most popular classics. Bargain stores, used book stores, and garage sales are also a great place to look. Remember that for early readers, the pictures may be as much of the fun as the text.

As your grandchildren grow older, you can begin to share more and more of your favorite books with them, such as a book you especially enjoyed reading when you were their age or a book you recently read that struck you as being of special interest.

There is no need to limit yourself to storybooks. A high schooler may want a good dictionary, and a university student may want a thesaurus. An encyclopedia can make a nice present for the family (remember that these are increasingly available on CD-ROM).

While we are on the topic of reading material, don't forget about magazines and comic books. A subscription to a magazine makes a wonderful present. Whether it is a magazine of puzzles, one about sports, or a fan magazine for a particular show or performer, a magazine as a gift serves as a weekly or monthly reminder that you care and are aware of their interests. After you have arranged for the subscription, make sure that the magazine is arriving regularly; when the time for renewal comes, talk with your grandchild. She may want to

pay for the renewal herself or replace it with another magazine.

I know that comic books are probably not most parents' and
grandparents' idea of reading material. Many of them are
pretty silly, and recently the classic superheroes have given
way to rather gruesome figures that have spin-offs in video
games, toys, and even movies. However, comic books can
instill a love of reading, and that's probably better than *not*
reading.

Computer Games and CD-ROMs

I have discussed some of the reasons to get over your com-
puterphobia in Chapter 6, on long-distance grandparenting.
Fortunately, you don't have to understand too much about
computers to pick out computer games for your grandchildren. If you know a few details about the computer they own,
the salesperson can guide you to the appropriate software.

One important word of warning: Be sure you check with the
parents. Many of today's CDs portray very graphic violence or
sexual imagery and may not be appropriate for all (or any) age
groups. Do not let this scare you off. There are many marvelous educational CDs and lots of others that are loads of fun
for all ages. There are games that teach colors and basic math
and spelling (for the youngest) and others that teach science,
history, geography, and astronomy for older children. Ency-
clopedias on CD-ROM include not only written text but also
music, sound, and video clips.

Sporting Equipment: Not Just for the Grandson!

If you're like me, you can remember when you could go into
a store and ask for sneakers without specifying whether they

were for cross-training, running, walking, or tennis—and without spending over a hundred dollars. You may also remember when "sporting equipment" meant, almost by definition, gifts for grandsons: baseball gloves, football helmets, and basketballs.

Things have changed. The sporting goods industry today is one of our country's most developed and trendiest industries and caters almost equally well to both males and females. The success of women's sports—both the traditional ones, such as figure skating, gymnastics, swimming, and field hockey, and what were once considered to be men's sports, such as soccer, basketball, and softball—has created a tremendous demand for equipment and wonderful opportunities for gift-giving. Do not be trapped by gender stereotypes in shopping for sporting equipment (or any other gift, for that matter). It has been a long time since girls worried about being called tomboys, and with the growing number of athletic scholarships available to women, a basketball could be not only fun but a good investment. If your granddaughter is into sports, share her passion and support it with a gift, just as you would for your grandson.

Another area in which sporting equipment has advanced greatly in recent years is safety. Although few of us would have considered wearing a helmet when riding a bicycle or roller skating, protection for the head, knees, and elbows is common today and is strongly recommended by experts in sports medicine. When buying gifts such as bikes, skateboards, or in-line skates, ask about the required safety equipment. Not only will this make your gift complete, but it will also mean that your granddaughter can use the gift as soon as she gets it and won't have to wait until her parents buy a helmet or pads.

Some sports, such as skiing, martial arts, and rock climbing, require not only equipment but also lessons. Lessons also make wonderful gifts, whether for beginners or for advanced sportsmen and sportswomen.

Oldies but Goodies: Board Games, Card Games, and Puzzles

In this era of computer games, CD-ROMs, and video arcades, low-tech items such as Candyland, Monopoly, and Sorry may not seem like very "in" gifts, but certain games seem immune to the passage of time. Many parents and grandparents like card games and board games because they don't include graphic violence, they do involve face-to-face interaction with other people, and they are relatively inexpensive. Not only do these low-tech games make excellent presents, but they're also good to have around the house for when your grandchildren visit. A number of families I know first introduced their children to these games when on vacation. Even though they could take their laptop computer with them when they traveled, many families prefer not to. Deprived of their favorite computer games, the children were forced to sit around the table and play Clue, Scrabble, or some other game—and before long they were hooked. (Many games come in special travel versions, which make excellent gifts before a trip or vacation.) Whether they have card games, board games, chess, or checkers, many families have sat around on rainy or snowy days and whiled away the hours talking, playing, drinking hot chocolate, or snacking.

Different games are suitable for different ages; usually the game box offers a good guide. There is a risk that your grandchildren will enjoy the game more than you do, and you'll find yourself stuck playing what seem like endless games of War,

Fish, and Chutes and Ladders, but it's a small price to pay for the hours of time shared.

Some families prefer, especially for the younger children, games that involve comparatively little skill and lots of luck. As your grandchildren get older, a mix of luck and skill can be fun. One grandmother I know taught her grandson to play bridge, and he sometimes plays with her and her cronies when he visits. It also provides them with a topic of conversation as she fills him in on her weekly games. A grandfather who enjoyed chess taught his granddaughter the basics of the game. Not only can they play on visits, but they exchange reports on important matches and discuss the results.

Puzzles are another old favorite that can be fun for all ages. Small children often begin with puzzles that have only a few large pieces, while preteens often like large jigsaw puzzles, the more pieces the better.

Camping Equipment

Even if you're not the outdoors type, your children and grandchildren may be. A sleeping bag is an especially versatile gift. Younger children may use it when they have a sleepover party or to camp out in the backyard. Older children may need a sleeping bag if they go to summer camp or when they go backpacking. Tents are also useful and come in many sizes. I have already mentioned knapsacks, but it bears repeating.

If you yourself enjoy hiking, rafting, camping, and other outdoor activities, you may not only give the gifts but you may get to share in the experience of using them. A family camping trip or hike can be a wonderful way to get together away from the noise and distractions of traffic, television, and work. Provided that sites and activities are planned to be appropriate for all ages, it can be a marvelous change of pace. You may also want to host such a trip by making the arrangements, planning the trip, and paying for the site fees.

Music: Instruments, Lessons, Concerts

Although music is one of the areas in which the generation gap is most pronounced, it is possible to build bridges over this gap through a variety of different gifts. Children are exposed to popular music through the radio and television at an earlier and earlier age, but there still is a period when the big hits are the many children's songs available on CD or cassette. These are wonderful presents not only for listening to at home but also for the car stereo on trips.

Although I still like the image of the entire family listening to the same music or singing songs as they set out on a vacation or drive to visit the grandparents, I know this is often not the case. The sound of the radio or tape may be drowned out by the arguments over what station to tune to, what cassette to play, and how loud to play it. A gift of a portable cassette or CD player may be particularly welcomed and will spare everyone the arguments over what station to listen to or what music to play. Although it may not be a classic picture of the happy family on the road, two teens, each listening to their favorites on a separate player, sure beats two screaming voices complaining the whole trip!

As your grandchildren get older, their musical taste will probably begin to diverge from yours a great deal. Keep an open mind. Remember that *your* parents and grandparents probably thought that Sinatra, Elvis, the Beatles, and Bob Dylan were pretty outrageous when you listened to them. In any event, you don't have to like their music to buy them presents. Very few teens own all the albums they want, and new ones are released at such a pace that you can almost always find a good gift choice.

One recent trend has been to label CDs and tapes to indicate that parental discretion is recommended because of the explicit content of the lyrics. Since this is a warning but not a prohibition, many authorities believe it serves to attract more teens than it deters. If you find such a label on the album your grandson has requested, be sure you clear it with his parents before you hand it over.

There are few gifts that give as much pleasure and can have as great an impact over the years as musical instruments. Whether it's a guitar, violin, flute, or saxophone, a musical instrument is perhaps the best example of a gift that has a ripple effect, bringing pleasure not only to the immediate recipient but over the course of time to others as well. I am not suggesting that you rush out to buy your grandson a piano because you want to hear him play. And only someone looking for trouble would buy her granddaughter a drum set without first clearing it with her parents. But I am a firm believer in *encouraging* children's love of music. Many schools have programs through which children are able to get their first instrument at minimal cost, but the purchase of a new instrument is usually the next step.

The gift of music often requires not only the purchase of an instrument, but months and, in many cases, years of lessons. Many parents balk at taking on this kind of long-term commitment, especially since it often involves a great deal of travel to and from teachers' homes or studios. They may be more at ease if you commit yourself to helping defray the costs of lessons or if you live close enough to share the carpooling.

Finally, you may want to treat your grandchild to concert tickets. If it is your kind of music, you can make it a shared outing. But even if it is not your style, concert tickets are so expensive today, that they will doubtless be a welcome gift.

Money

In many ways, money is the easiest gift to give. One size fits all, you don't have to worry if they will like it, it is easy to send by mail, and it certainly doesn't go out of style. If money is a fad, it is one of the longest and most successful.

The only problem with giving money is that many people feel that it is just too impersonal. If the only gift you ever send is a check, the message you may be sending is that you don't really want to be bothered thinking about what would be a good present or you don't know your grandchild well enough to make even an informed guess. Be careful that money is not the *only* present you ever give, and keep track so that you don't fall into the habit of giving money instead of other gifts.

With a bit of creative thinking, money can be as personal a gift as any other. For example, if your grandson is saving up to buy a guitar, a contribution to the fund will be welcomed and shows that you are aware and supportive of his plans. (A quick conversation with his parents will also help you judge how large a gift is appropriate, given his plans and needs and their expectations.) A gift certificate to a particular store that sells books, CDs, games, and the like, is also a way of combining the ease of a cash gift with an expression of personal interest. Gift certificates to a local movie theater are also appreciated. When you have given gift certificates be sure to inquire about the CDs, books, or movies that your grandchildren bought or viewed—not to check up on them but to learn more for the next time you want to give a gift.

I know that one reason many grandparents don't like to give money is that they are afraid that their grandchild will just waste it. Assuming that you are not giving your grandchildren large sums that they are too young to appreciate (and if you are, you need to reexamine your gift-giving policy), the worst that can happen is that they learn the valuable lesson about a fool and his money. It is perfectly acceptable to ask your grandson what he did with the money you gave him, but like any other gift, the money belongs to the recipient. A friend of mine in his forties still remembers his grandfather's disdain when he spent a dollar on comic books and baseball cards. Another friend's teenage son bought a cellular phone with his gift money. After a few months he was pretty tired of it, but he never heard an "I told you so" and never expressed any regrets. The lesson is not to spoil your gift by being a gift critic.

Some grandparents open bank accounts for their grandchildren and add to them on birthdays and special occasions. Shares of stock may not sound like a very interesting gift, but owning a piece of Toys R Us or Hershey's could be rather exciting and would be a fun introduction to the world of investing and finance. More serious forms of such gifts are trust funds, for which you should consult a financial expert. I think it's wonderful to set aside money in this way, but remember that it's not a substitute for more immediate and more personal gifts.

Thank You

There was a time when it was assumed that every gift would be followed by a handwritten and personal thank-you note.

Today, many grandparents (and others) report they would be gratified just to receive, whether in writing or over the phone, a simple "Thank you." Unfortunately, the failure to acknowledge gifts is not limited to grandchildren. The writing of thank-you notes, like most aspects of good manners and etiquette, is something that children learn at home from their parents and others around them. If your grandchildren don't write to thank you for a gift (or mention it the next time you call), it probably means that their parents haven't taught them the importance of such simple gestures. Don't be embarrassed to mention this to your children.

If you have developed a pattern of letter writing (whether by e-mail or regular "snailmail") with your grandchildren, you probably have a better chance of receiving either a special thank-you note or at least a thank-you in the next mailing you receive. Regular conversations may also provide an opportunity. However, if you don't hear anything, there is no reason to be shy; just ask if the gift arrived and, if it has, whether they liked it.

Some grandparents have found an original and rather direct way to make sure their gift has arrived. They include a self-addressed stamped postcard with the gift. On the message side there is a checklist.

The gift arrived on: <u>month/day/year</u>

It was in good/bad condition

The thing I like most about it is _____

For younger children, it can be fun to fill out the card with their parents. Older children may not find the postcard very subtle, but at least you'll know whether or not the gift arrived.

Living Legacies

Thus far the gifts I have spoken about have been moderately expensive and intended as special treats. If you are so inclined and the resources you have permit it, you may wish to give larger, more substantial gifts. These might include money for a down payment on a house, tuition for private school or college, property, or a car.

One of the dilemmas you inevitably face with such gifts involves the issue of fairness. Although some families find it easiest to give equal amounts to each of their grandchildren, even this is not as simple as it sounds. College tuition can vary by thousands of dollars from school to school or state to state. The same is true of housing prices. In some areas that still have excellent public schools, private school is a luxury; elsewhere it may be the only option for a proper education. Paying for tuition for your single-parent grandchildren may mean the difference between their attending a first-rate school or not, while for the child of a corporate lawyer–father and a physician-mother, it may simply provide the parents with disposable income they hadn't expected to have.

Given my own experience and the values with which I was raised, education has always seemed to be one of the finest gifts anyone can give. It sends a clear message of the importance you attach to education and is also a gift that seeks to help your grandchild on his way to professional and personal success and financial independence. College costs today are so high that all but the wealthiest of families find it difficult to send one child, not to speak of several, through school. Moreover, the costs have continued to rise faster than either the rate of inflation or the average salary. Even two-career families in which both parents are professionals find it hard to afford the tuition at private colleges and universities. One-parent families usually find it impossible, and unfortunately many scholarship packages of grants and loans fall far short of students' real needs.

9

Families in Many
Shapes and Sizes

You hear a lot of dialogue on the death of the American family.
Families aren't dying. They're merging into big conglomerates.

Erma Bombeck, *San Francisco Examiner*, October 1, 1978

There was a time when everyone knew or at least thought they
knew what a family was. A father, a mother, and a couple of
children was the image that immediately leapt to mind and
was strongly promoted on television and in the print media.
Grandparents, if acknowledged at all, were in the distant background. Not only were racially or religiously mixed families
invisible, but nonwhite families were rarely if ever depicted.
Single parents, divorcees, blended families, and gays and lesbians were taboo subjects. While many people today still carry
with them a very specific picture of what a family is, there is
also a much greater realization that families come in every
imaginable shape and size.

It is not surprising that the vast majority of television depictions of family diversity are comedies. (The superb drama "Party of Five" is a notable exception.) One cannot help but wonder if the popularity of such programs ("Step-by-Step," "Full House," "Murphy Brown") among television executives is as much the result of the possibilities they offer for humor and bizarre situations as of any desire to do justice to modern family life.

One of the problems with such shows—and to an even greater degree with many of the books available about nontraditional families—is that however good their intentions, they often unwittingly pathologize the families they portray. In other words, they treat them not first and foremost as families—a group of people linked together by some combination of love, commitment, cohabitation, bloodlines, and memories—but as *a problem.* Indeed, many of the books for children about divorce, adoption, and stepparents, however admirable their intentions and positive the message they seek to convey, all too often fall into the problem/solution genre. The characters are faced with criticism or rejection because of their unusual situation—the problem; they and others come to learn acceptance—the solution. Thus, when they appear, single parents are primarily portrayed as *single* (the problem) and only as an afterthought as *parents,* adopted children are *adopted* and then *children,* and gay couples are *gay* and then *couples.* Even today, it is almost unheard of to have a single parent, gay parent, or adopted child as a character in a book that is *not* about the specifics of their situation.

By including a special section on some special types of families in this book, it is not my intention to continue this approach. The family arrangements discussed in this chapter are not oddities, curiosities, or problems. Nor are they particularly rare. These situations encompass millions of children, parents, and grandchildren. All the parents discussed here share most of the same concerns as the parents discussed in the rest of the book. All the children considered in this chapter are first and foremost *children*. And perhaps most important, being a grandparent to your grandchildren is not so different regardless of the family setting they live in. You will have to decide the role(s) you wish to fill, the gifts you wish to share, and the traditions you wish to pass on. Nevertheless, each of the families described in this chapter presents special concerns and challenges of which you as a grandparent should be aware.

The Chosen Child

In Chapter 1, I talked a little bit about those grandparents who feel that they've achieved that status too quickly. Others, however, feel that they've had to wait forever. This is often the result of a couple's decision to postpone parenting until they have finished school or are more established professionally. As much as you may not like it, you have to accept their decision.

In other cases, the delay may be because they are having trouble conceiving a child of their own. Not too long ago, such couples had few options. But medical science has made great progress in fertility treatment, and more and more couples have conceived after receiving treatment in clinics or hospitals. For those who find no medical solution, there are a variety of other options. In some cases, such as with donated sperm, the child may share the biological heritage of his mother or, when donor eggs are used, of his father.

Others decide to adopt. Surprisingly, there are no definitive data regarding the number of children adopted by nonfamily members in America today. In 1986 the National Committee for Adoption reported in its *Encyclopedia of Adoption* that during that year there were about 105,000 adoptions, more or less evenly split between adoptions by relatives and adoptions by strangers. This figure is a single-year total, not a cumulative figure. According to the U.S Bureau of the Census, in 1991, 1.1 million children under age eighteen were living with an adoptive parent. Of this number, 581,000 (55 percent) lived with two adoptive parents, 31 percent lived with one adoptive parent and one biological parent, and 12 percent lived with a single parent. These figures include adoptions by aunts, uncles, and grandparents and represent about 2 percent of all children, but they do not include adoptees who are adults today. H. David Kirk, the author of several works on adoption, wrote in 1984: "Assuming a low figure of five million adoptees, that figure can be multiplied by eight . . . [if we consider parents, grandparents, aunts and uncles, so that] one fifth of the people are directly or intimately linked to the experience of adoption." This is yet further evidence of how widespread a phenomenon can be and still not be part of most people's view of a typical family. Both the number and percentage of adopted children has declined over the past two decades. Most authorities agree that this is the result of liberalized abortion laws and an increase in the number of unwed mothers who decide to keep their babies.

If your children decide to adopt because of their inability to have biological offspring, there are a number of things you should keep in mind about their needs. Infertility treatments themselves are invasive and frustrating and place a great strain on many couples. Most couples turn to adoption only after years of pursuing different paths to having their own child.

Adoption itself is also a difficult and expensive process. Although agencies are certainly justified in screening applicants carefully, potential parents often comment bitterly on the endless forms they must fill out and questions they must answer in order to have a child. They often complain that they are being put through the wringer to achieve something that, in many cases, any two people can do: have a child to raise.

Even after being approved for adoption, the process can be nerve-wracking. In some cases, parents wait anxiously, fearful that the birth parents might renege and decide at the last minute to keep the child. In others, there is little advance notice when a child becomes available, and they become instant parents.

Healthy, white newborns are in great demand among adoptive parents, and there are far too few of them to meet this demand. Since some agencies within the United States also oppose interracial adoptions, many parents go outside the country to adopt. Foreign adoptions involve the risks of a strange bureaucracy, and on some occasions eager potential parents have been victimized by unscrupulous agencies.

At the least, adoption means that you and your children will be denied the experience of pregnancy, preparation, and childbirth. However, as I will discuss further in the next chapter, the trend toward open adoptions has offered, for at least some adoptive parents, the possibility of getting to know the birthparents and being involved in the birth process.

Some grandparents are afraid (as in the case of stepgrandchildren) that they won't be able to really love a child who is not their biological descendant, especially if she is racially different. In most cases, these concerns evaporate quickly. Countless grandparents report that their reservations were swept away the first time they held their new grandchild.

It is helpful to remember that in many cultures, a grandparent is not necessarily a blood relative. In China, for example, an aging woman with no close kin could be adopted by a couple. She would have the same relationship and responsibilities of reciprocity as a blood mother and grandmother. There are also many reports of how, in the absence of a caregiver, a stranger would adopt not only the role of grandmother but the name as well. Closer to home, generations of African-American women have been "grandmother" to nieces, nephews, cousins, and even children with whom they had no blood relationship.

Adopted children usually have special concerns of their own. For many, being chosen can also carry with it the possibility of being unchosen. Others feel a special pressure to live up to being chosen. No matter how supportive and loving a child's parents may be, there will be times when adoptees identify with the social conventions that parents and grandparents are those with whom you share a blood relationship. Often this happens during the teen years, when many an angry child rebels against parental authority. For parents who have cared and nurtured a child for his whole life, nothing is more hurtful than being told, "You can't tell me what to do, you're not even my real father." At times like this, a grandparent may prove to be a valuable mediator, reminding both teen and parents of the love, affection, and memories they share: "You are their child, and they are your parents."

Every chosen child is also, it must be remembered, a surrendered child. Although most adoptees learn something about the circumstances of their adoption from their parents, this is rarely sufficiently detailed or emotionally satisfying. Many fantasize about their "real" parents, and it is not uncommon for adopted children to search for their birthparents. In closed adoptions, this can be extremely difficult, and authorities may not be willing or legally able to assist. These days, however, the search for one's parents is often a comparatively simple process, at least on the technical level. Even today, however, most of the assistance and counseling available are offered to the child, not to the family. Adoptive parents are often deeply threatened by their child's search for his biological parents, and here, too, you may have an important role to play as counselor to both your children and your grandchildren.

You will, of course, have to follow your children's lead as to when and what to tell your grandchild about the circumstances of her adoption. (Remember, that includes talking to your other grandchildren about their new sibling or cousin.) The same is also true for issues such as cultural heritage.

One thing that you should always keep in mind as the grandparent of a chosen child is just how much your children wanted to be parents. In most cases, they have struggled through not only medical difficulties but administrative and bureaucratic intrusions. There were probably many times when they were plunged into despair. If they are like the adoptive parents I know, all of that has made them treasure their children even more. And so should you!

Gay and Lesbian Couples

Since the 1980s, when I first became well known as "Dr. Ruth," I have received many calls and letters from listeners who are gays or lesbians. I have also counseled many homosexual couples who have been together for years. I have found that the problems they confront are generally the same problems confronted by any two partners in a sexual relationship. Given the prejudices they encounter and the difficulties they continue to face in legalizing their unions, life is more difficult for homosexual partners than for other couples. Often these difficulties are not limited to the broader society but involve their immediate families as well.

Homosexuals frequently find it difficult to get their families to accept their lifestyle and their partners. Although this also happens to heterosexual couples, particularly in interfaith and interracial marriages, for gays and lesbians the objection usually is not only to the particular partner but to their sexual orientation as a whole.

Even those parents who have come to terms with their children's sexual orientation often continue to express distress at being denied the chance to be grandparents. Although in the past it was generally assumed that gay and lesbian households were childless, one of the important changes that has taken place in the past two decades is that a growing number of gay and lesbian couples are raising children. Some cases involve divorced women who are raising their children with their lesbian partners. In other cases, lesbian couples have had children through artificial insemination. Although it is rarer for gay men to raise children, it does take place, either with children from previous marriages or by adoption.

According to one recent article, gay and lesbian couples account for about 5 percent of families in the United States. In 1990, the editors of the *Harvard Law Review* reported that "approximately three million gay men and lesbians in the

United States are parents, and between eight and ten million children are raised in gay or lesbian households." The vast majority of these children were born in heterosexual unions before their parents' coming out, others were conceived through artificial insemination, and others were adopted. An estimated 10,000 lesbians have borne children. The recent New Jersey court decision approving an adoption by two gay men will doubtless lead to an increase in these numbers.

I know that many people are appalled by the idea of homosexuals, whether men or women, having anything to do with children, much less raising them. Women who have had children and then divorced often face bitter custody battles with their husbands when they reveal their interest in female sexual partners.

The case that has gotten the most headlines and is of the most relevance to this book occurred in Virginia in 1993, when Kay Bottoms petitioned to have her then two-year-old grandson taken away from his mother, Sharon Bottoms, simply because Sharon Bottoms is a lesbian. The court granted the petition, giving custody to Kay Bottoms. The Virginia Supreme Court upheld this decision in June 1994, but the case has yet to be heard by the U.S. Supreme Court. Until it is, the boy remains separated from his mother.

This is absurd. The fact is that sentiments against gay parents are precisely that—sentiments. Some people don't *like* the idea of a little boy being raised by two moms, but no scientific study has ever shown any psychological ill effects on children raised by gay parents, nor (and this is the fear that lies under the surface) any effect on the children's sexual orientation. In fact, as John Laird's recent overview of research on gay and lesbian parents shows, "a generation of research has failed to demonstrate that gays or lesbians are any less fit to parent than their heterosexual counterparts. . . . [studies] have failed to produce any evidence that children of lesbian or gay parents are harmed or compromised." A New Jersey appellate court suggested that children raised by lesbian or gay parents might "emerge better equipped to search out their own standards of right and wrong, better able to perceive that the majority is not always correct in its moral judgments, and better able to understand the importance of conforming their beliefs to requirements of reason and tested knowledge, not the constraints of currently popular sentiment or prejudice."

Clearly, what is important for a child is being raised by a parent—or better yet, parents—who love and can provide for him or her. We will never bolster the family if we insist that it has to fit the old-fashioned and, in many cases, outdated model. Our definition of family *has* to include a prominent role not only for grandparents (and fathers and stepfamilies) but also for gays and lesbians.

My feeling is that because they really have to overcome obstacles in order to bear and/or raise children and because the tragedy of AIDS has given them a heightened awareness of the need to affirm and continue life, gay people, in the majority of cases, make *exceptional* parents.

I know that is the case with a woman named Julie, a hospital administrator, who is raising two children with her partner Ellen, a lawyer. After they had been together nine years, Julie was artificially inseminated and gave birth to Katie. Three years later, it was Ellen's turn, and she gave birth to Max. The kids call both mothers Mom, switching to Julie or Ellen if further clarification is needed.

Julie and Ellen realize the importance of male role models,

especially for Max. "Ellen's parents moved from New York to Philadelphia when Katie was one and a half," Julie says, "and their grandfather is very important in both kids' lives."

Although it is hard to generalize from a single case, I think Julie and Ellen's situation supports some of the suggestions made in Chapter 4 about grandfathers. Given the large number of families that are headed by females (either single mothers or lesbians), grandfathers have a special role to play in the modern family. In saying this, it is by no means my intention to belittle the efforts and achievements of these mothers. (Grandmothers have a similar role to play in families with no woman present.) I merely wish to point out that if both sexes have something vital to give to the education of our children, men, far more often than women, are the absent element.

Interfaith Families

In Jewish families, intermarriage has traditionally been every parent's worst nightmare. In the past, it was not uncommon for families to go into mourning, as if the child who married out of the faith had died. Tevye, the philosophic milkman in *Fiddler on the Roof*, is able to accept two of his daughters' marriage choices but balks when a third marries a Christian. Scarcely a month goes by without some Jewish organization publishing alarming figures about the high rates of intermarriage among Jews in America. In 1960, only about 5 percent of Jews intermarried. Today the figure is closer to a third, and some claim even higher figures. One recent survey indicated that American Jews today view intermarriage, rather than anti-Semitism, as the greatest threat to Jewish life in the United States. Some, engaging in a comparison of dubious validity and even poorer taste, call intermarriage in America a "second Holocaust."

Others have decided, whatever their feelings, to attempt to accommodate themselves to this new reality, as witnessed in the book by Sunie Levin, *Mingled Roots: A Guide for Jewish Grandparents of Interfaith Grandchildren.*

Although I have far less firsthand familiarity with their circumstances, my general impression is that American Muslims are also overwhelmingly opposed to intermarriage. In the word's of one *imam* (religious leader), "When you are living in America, you are up against so many pressures, so many influences of the society which are un-Islamic, and the father and mother are the only hope for the children's maintaining their identity as Muslims or knowing about their religion." In general Muslims are more tolerant of intermarriage by men, since it is believed that the father will see to it that his children are raised as Muslims. In contrast, it is assumed that a Muslim woman who marries a non-Muslim will have to raise her children in her husband's faith. Although this may be the case in Muslim countries, it can by no means be taken for granted in the United States. Although many Muslim parents would prefer that their daughters not marry at all rather than marry outside their faith, nevertheless, American-born Muslims—both men and women—do marry non-Muslims. In most cases, their parents strongly oppose such marriages and, at the least, try to convince their sons-in-law to convert and permit their grandchildren be raised as Muslims.

Not all groups share the Jewish and Muslim dread of intermarriage. Surveys indicate that intermarriages between Protestants and Catholics have increased dramatically in the second half of this century. Nevertheless, most parents continue to prefer that their children marry someone "like us," either religiously, ethnically, or racially. Your child's decision to marry outside his faith may have caused dismay, embarrassment, and even a major crisis in family relations. However, by the time grandchildren come along, it is clearly time to move on. Many parents only come to terms with their child's choice of a partner when a grandchild is born. The sight of their grandchild seems to melt away all their misgivings or at least push them aside. The late writer Bernard Malamud recounted in an essay that his father sat shiva (the Jewish traditional way of mourning) when he married a Gentile wife. Nevertheless, Malamud recalled, "After the birth of our son, my father came gently to greet my wife and touch his grandchild."

Despite this and other examples, I certainly would not recommend that you wait for your grandchild to arrive to patch up any differences you have had with your children over their choice of spouse. As I have already discussed, establishing good relations with your in-laws is one of the most important steps in building a strong connection with your grandchildren. You can never reclaim the years you will have lost. When I see families feuding, whatever the reason, I wonder if they realize how lucky they are to have family members at all. Many of us would give up everything we have for just a few minutes with our departed loved ones, regardless of their previous faults or failings, real or imagined. If despite the passage of time and the birth of a grandchild you still cannot share your child's joy with his spouse and children, at least have the good sense and courtesy not to cast a cloud over their celebration.

Perhaps the first question that all intermarried couples are asked, whether out of curiosity or under the peculiar assumption that they have not considered it, is "What about the children? How are you going to raise them?"

Whatever *your* preferences may be, such decisions are those of the parents. They may decide to raise their children in one of their traditions, in a combination of the two, or in neither. Often the birth of the first child and decisions about a brit, christening, or other religious ceremony will bring to the surface questions that have previously been relegated to the background. Whatever they decide regarding this and other similar situations, you must at least respect their wishes. Ideally, of course, it is best to discuss this with them as you would any other aspect of their approach to raising their children. Try to learn and understand as much you can about their approach. If you discuss these issues in a general way before specific questions arise, everyone should be less tense and defensive.

Of course, your concern for their wishes does not mean that you must abandon, hide, or compromise your heritage. Your traditions and your pride in your roots are a major part of who you are, and you have every right to share them in that context. If your children wish to visit you on special holidays, make it clear that you will be celebrating and exactly what that means on a practical level. Similarly, make clear the limits that you are willing to tolerate in the celebration of other customs. Just as you would indicate that you do not allow smoking in your house or ask that they respect your vegetarianism, you can indicate what foods will be tolerated or what customs of other faiths are acceptable. When you travel to visit your children, you must respect their house rules as well. Do not expect them to change their method of celebrating (or not) to make you comfortable.

If it is any comfort, such issues are not limited to intermarried couples. They also occur when children join new religious groups or when parents and children disagree regarding their level of observance within a religious tradition.

Interracial/Interethnic Families

Having lived in Israel, France, and for most of my adult life in the United States, I am no stranger to the ethnic and cultural diversity of the population in each of those countries and throughout the world. Israelis, so the saying goes, love immigration but dislike immigrants. Americans, too, love to talk about diversity but dislike people who are different. We have always been a nation of immigrants or, in the case of most Africans who reached our shores, forced migrants. Even so, the past decade and half has seen a dramatic transformation of the American population. In 1980, whites (that is non-Hispanic whites) of all religions and ethnic backgrounds made up 80 percent of all Americans. Today the number is 74 percent. At the same time, the proportion of blacks has declined slightly, from 13 to 12 percent. In contrast, the percentage of Asians or Pacific islanders has doubled from 2 to 4 percent, and Hispanics have increased from 6 to 11 percent in 1997. When it is remembered that each percentage point represents over 2.7 million people, these figures are truly significant. According to figures recently released, in mid-1997 almost 10 percent of those living in the United States were not born in this country. In 1970, non-natives made up less than 5 percent of the population.

It is not surprising that the percentage of marriages between racial groups has also grown appreciably in recent years. Only just over thirty years ago, in 1967, did the Supreme Court strike down as unconstitutional the remaining state laws out-lawing such marriages. According to the Census Bureau there were three times as many (337,000) black/white married couples in America in 1996 as there were in 1980. Interracial marriages in general more than doubled from 651,000 in 1980 to almost 1.4 million in 1995. Sixty-five percent of Japanese-Americans marry spouses with no Japanese ancestors, and 70 percent of Native Americans intermarry. In both of these groups, the number of children born in the United States to mixed couples outnumbers those born to uni-ethnic couples. Interethnic marriages between members of European ethnic groups are probably too numerous to document but vary between 50 to 80 percent of all marriages. Under the circumstances, it is hardly surprising that census officials are finding the existing very broad categories to be almost obsolete.

Unless you have lived in rather unusual circumstances, whenever you daydreamed about your future grandchildren, you almost certainly assumed that they would belong, if not to your ethnic group, at least to your racial group. The interracial marriage of your child and the birth of your grandchild put an end to that particular vision.

Given the difficulties interracial couples still face in America today, you have every right to be concerned for your children. They will doubtless be the subject of unkind remarks and slights from both sides of the racial divide. Initially, most couples are concerned about the responses of those closest to them: parents, siblings, grandparents, and close friends. Here as elsewhere, I hope you can find it in your heart to support your children in their choice.

In contrast to interfaith families, interracial couples have comparatively little choice regarding how people identify their children. Every ethnic group has its own traditions and customs, and parents can decide to emphasize the particular heritage of one group, both, or neither. However, nonfamily members will usually identify a child's ancestry on the basis of various (often inaccurate) aspects of her appearance or make assumptions (often unwarranted) based on her ancestry.

Under the peculiar logic of American racial categories, for example, a child with one black parent usually is usually considered to be black. (Under what was historically known as the one-drop rule; in the not too distant past, a person with *any* black ancestors was classified as black.) Not only is this not the case in most other countries, it is not the case in America with regard to mixed Asian-European children.

Without going too far into the dynamics of race relations in the United States today, I think I can safely say that most white people have only the most superficial understanding of what life is like for most black people in the United States. One of the most powerful statements on the effect of racism in America today was made in 1992 by the African-American tennis star, Arthur Ashe. Frail and dying of AIDS but as soft-spoken and dignified as ever, Ashe was asked by a reporter for *People* magazine if dealing with AIDS was the most difficult experience of his life. No, Ashe replied, AIDS was not the most difficult experience—being black was. And this was from a wealthy, successful, and widely respected personality.

What I am trying to say here is that if one of your grandchild's parents is of a different race or ethnic group, she may face challenges and problems that are completely unfamiliar to you. Whether these are positive stereotypes (like an expectation that Asian Americans will be good in math and science) or negative ones, you may be confronted with some new and not necessarily enjoyable experiences. One white grandmother I know who lives in a prosperous suburban neighborhood went into a local store with her teenage grandson whose father is African-American. She told him to wait for a minute while she picked something up. Imagine her dismay when the store owner, whom she'd known for years, approached her grandson and demanded to know what he was doing in the store.

Some of these unpleasant surprises can be avoided if you form a close relationship with your son-in-law or daughter-in-law. Hearing from her about her own experiences growing up in a different culture will almost certainly sensitize you to some of the issues your grandchild may face. Learning about the grandparenting traditions of your in-laws is also almost always an enriching experience. In any event, it's important that your grandson understand at an early age that whatever the attitudes of others, you are his ally; and whatever your differences in background or appearance, your love and support are unconditional.

Special Needs

There are few things more shocking to a parent or grandparent than the birth of a child with special physical, mental, or emotional problems. When we looked into the future and imagined our grandchildren, we always assumed that they would be perfect in every way. It is not easy to come back down to earth and accept the reality of a grandchild whose appearance or potential achievement is of a totally different type. Many grandparents feel disappointed, resentful, and embarrassed. Do not hesitate to discuss these feelings with a friend or a professional (although not, of course, with the parents). For many people, knowledge is a powerful weapon in the fight against despair and fear of the unknown. Try to find out as much as you can about your new grandchild's situation and the resources and opportunities available for her and her family.

Remember, whether your grandchild has a hearing impairment or an emotional problem, a learning disability or a debilitating disease, she is a special child and needs your love as much as any of your other grandchildren. Although we have passed the day when such children were routinely locked away or, even worse, left to die, our high-pressured, competitive society is a hostile setting for the disadvantaged. Despite such legislation as the Americans with Disabilities Act, equal opportunity is still only a dream for many.

What can you do? As a parent, you have a special role to play in supporting your children—your grandchild's parents. They will need understanding and compassion to get over the shock and accept their new reality. Do not be surprised if there is a period of denial or self-blame or even mutual recriminations as to whose "fault" it is. Help them acknowledge their new situation.

On a practical level, parents of special children often find the day-to-day responsibilities exhausting and readily welcome any relief. Anything that you can do to help your children maintain their normal routine or get a respite from their daily tasks will help both them and your grandchild.

Even if you're not living nearby, you can be a source of support and comfort. Parents are often so overwhelmed with the day-to-day tasks of caring for their special-needs child that they have no time to keep track of new information or engage in advocacy. By affiliating with an organization that promotes the cause of children like your grandchild, you do both.

To cite only one example: The past two decades have seen tremendous advances in our understanding of learning disabilities and behavioral disorders such as ADD (attention deficit disorder). Tens and even hundreds of thousands of children who only a short while ago were being dismissed as difficult or slow are now being helped. Often it is a grandparent who is the first to suggest that a meeting with a professional might be of service to both the child and the parents.

Your special-needs grandchild may never have the sort of life you dreamed of for her, but with your help and love she may achieve things that will fill your heart with a warmth and pride you might never have imagined.

There are so many different kinds of families today, and this chapter can only mention some of the more common types found in the late 1990s. Moreover, each of the families described here may skip a generation. It may be your *grandchild* who intermarries, adopts a child, or raises your great-grandchild with a same-sex partner. Hopefully, you will be able to cherish them and their parents as much as ever as they build your bridge into the future.

Further Reading and Resources

ADAMEC, CHRISTINE, and WILLIAM L. PIERCE. *The Encyclopedia of Adoption* (New York: Facts on File, 1991).

ASHTON, JOYCE, with DENNIS ASHTON. *Loss and Grief Recovery: Help Caring for Children with Disabilities, Chronic or Terminal Illness* (Amityville, NY: Baywood Publishing, 1996).

BARRETT, ROBERT L., and BRYAN E. ROBINSON. *Gay Fathers* (Lexington, MA: Lexington Books, 1990).

Biracial Child Magazine
P.O. Box 12048
Atlanta, GA 30355-2048
404-364-9690

BOZETT, FREDERICK W., ed. *Gay and Lesbian Parents* (New York: Praeger, 1987).

Dovetail: A Journal by and for Jewish/Christian Families
485 Hauser Ave.
Holbrook, NY 11741
For a complete list of available publications, contact:
Dovetail Publishing, Inc.,
P.O. Box 19945
Kalamazoo, MI 49019
Tel. 616-342-2900
www.mich.com/~dovetail
dovetail@mich.com

Federation of Parents and Friends of Lesbian and Gays (P-Flag)
P.O. Box 24565
Los Angeles, CA 90024
This group has chapters in major cities in the United States.

GOODMAN-MALAMUTH, LESLIE, and ROBIN MARGOLIS. *Between Two Worlds: Choices for Grown Children of Jewish-Christian Parents* (New York: Pocket Books, 1992).

GRUZEN, LEE F. *Raising Your Jewish/Christian Child* (New York: Newmarket Press, 1990).

HAWXHURST, JOAN C. *Bubbe & Gram: My Two Grandmothers* (Kalamazoo, MI: Dovetail Publishing, 1996).

LAIRD, JOHN, "Lesbian and Gay Families." In F. Walsh, Ed. *Normal Family Processes,* 2nd ed. (New York: Guilford, 1993), 282-328.

LEVIN, SUNIE. *Mingled Roots: A Guide for Jewish Grandparents of Interfaith Grandchildren* (Washington, DC: B'nai B'rith Women, 1991).

LEWIN, ELLEN. *Lesbian Mothers* (Ithaca, NY: Cornell University Press, 1993).

LINDSAY, JEANNE WARREN. *Open Adoption: A Caring Option* (Buena Park, CA: Morning Glory Press, 1987).

MILLER, NANCY B. *Nobody's Perfect: Living and Growing with Children Who Have Special Needs* (Baltimore: Paul H. Brookes, 1994).

National Council for Adoption
1930 Seventeenth Street, NW
Washington, DC 20009
202-328-1200

PAUL, ELLEN, Ed. *The Adoption Directory* (Detroit: Gale Research, 1989).

REUBEN, STEVEN CARR. *But How Will You Raise the Children?* (New York: Pocket Books, 1987).

ROMANO, DUGAN. *Intercultural Marriage: Promises & Pitfalls* (Yarmouth, ME: Intercultural Press, 1988). This and similar books are available from Intercultural Press, P.O. Box 768, Yarmouth, ME 04096.

ROSENBLATT, PAUL C., TERRI A. KARIS, and RICHARD D. POWELL. *Multiracial Couples* (Thousand Oaks, CA: Sage Publications, 1995).

SCHAFFER, JUDITH, and CHRISTINA LINDSTROM. *How to Raise an Adopted Child* (New York: Crown Publishers, 1989).

WASSERMAN, SELMA. *The Long-Distance Grandmother: How to Stay Close to Distant Grandchildren* (Point Robbins, WA: Hartley & Marks, 1990). Includes a chapter about grandchildren with special needs.

10

Going It Alone: Single-Parent Families

In 1995, only 69 percent of American children lived with both their parents. The other 31 percent lived with only their mothers (24 percent), fathers (3 percent), or neither parent (4 percent). In fact, these figures underestimate the place of the single-parent household in children's experience, because they offer a snapshot of a given moment in time rather than a picture of the dynamic cycle of family life. The U.S. Government estimates that 61 percent of children born in 1987 will spend some time in a single-parent household before they reach the age of eighteen.

Most single-parent households result from divorce, desertion, and death, topics covered in Chapters 11 and 12. In this chapter, I want to consider single-parent households that are the result of what we used to call illegitimate births: children born out of wedlock. I want to start out by making what I believe is an important distinction between children born to teens and those born to older unmarried women.

Teen Single Mothers: Children Raising Children

Few aspects of family life are more culturally determined than the ages of betrothal, marriage, and childbearing. We are all familiar with peoples among whom teen marriage and teenage mothers are not only common but the expected norm. One of the things that I discovered in the course of my research on Ethiopian Jews in Israel is that in Ethiopia, child betrothal was quite common and almost all women were married with children before the age of twenty. Indeed, the single Ethiopian women in their late teens and early twenties found in Israel today are the first generation of singles in that community. Closer to home, a careful look at many of our own family histories will usually reveal a grandparent or other relative who had her first child at age fifteen or sixteen.

Such comparisons are unfortunately misleading and should not be taken as evidence that today's teen mothers are following a long tradition. In many societies, women marry at a comparatively early age; thus teen mothers are also teen wives. In the 1950s and 1960s, a high percentage of the teenage mothers in America were married women. This is clearly not the case today.

Over the past thirty years, the average age at marriage has risen steadily. The median age of women at the time of their first marriage in 1970 was only 20.6. Even in 1980, almost a third of all first-time brides were under age twenty. By 1996, the median age had risen to 24.8, and 91.3 percent of all eighteen- and nineteen-year-old women had never been married. Although the number of children born to teenage mothers has actually declined during the past few decades, today these mothers are usually not married (in contrast to our own past and the experience of other societies).

In 1970, slightly less than 400,000 children were born to unwed mothers of all ages in the United States. By 1992, the number of babies born to unwed *teens* was 365,000. (The overall figure of births out of wedlock had skyrocketed to over 1.2 million!)

Although single motherhood is accurately perceived to be more common among blacks than whites, it actually has risen more dramatically for Caucasians during this period. In 1970, less than 6 percent of births to whites were illegitimate. By 1992, that number had risen to over 22 percent. (In comparison, illegitimacy among blacks rose from over 37 percent in 1970 to over 68 percent in 1992.)

Despite all these statistics, teen pregnancy continues to be something, like divorce, that most people assume happens in other people's families. When you first learn that your daughter is pregnant, you will probably be upset and confused. You may be asking yourself, "Where did I fail?" or asking your daughter, "How could you do this to *me*?" You may have feelings of shame: *No one must find out about this.* You may also have very set opinions about whether to give the child up for adoption or to keep and raise your grandchild, either by yourself or with your daughter.

One thing you should avoid doing is taking over and making a decision without taking your daughter into account. At first glance, the options available to your teenager and your family when faced with an unexpected pregnancy are pretty straightforward. They vary, however, with regard to long-term implications.

According to a survey published in 1994, the United States leads all developed countries in the incidence of teen pregnancies. Although some people claim that this is because our teens are more promiscuous than those elsewhere, this is not what the evidence indicates. Failed or unused birth control are the cause of these pregnancies. Accordingly, whatever decision you and your child make, it is crucial that you see to it that your child gets access to accurate information about birth control, and that once she *has* birth control she *uses* it.

During the Pregnancy

There are a number of practical issues to be considered while you're awaiting the birth of your grandchild. As usual, good communication with your child will make many things much easier. Very young mothers are almost twice as likely to have a low-birth-weight baby than older mothers. They also have a higher risk of having a premature baby with health problems. It is crucial, therefore, that you arrange for your daughter to get the best prenatal care possible.

Although you may hesitate to discuss your situation out of a sense of either embarrassment or shame, it is important that you not isolate yourself or your child from friends and family who can offer moral and practical support. If there are other children in the family, it is also vital that you keep them as fully informed as possible about their sister's condition and plans. The last thing that you want to happen is for them to hear about the situation from an outsider. Even the youngest children will probably sense that something unusual is going on. Older children and teens may find the situation even more difficult. The knowledge that a sister who they're especially close to has been sexual active and gotten pregnant can produce a wide range of reactions from embarrassment to anger and resentment. Do not neglect your other children because of your concern for your pregnant child.

Do not neglect yourself either. Although teen mothers usually have access to a variety of types of counseling, this is usually not the case with grandparents. Indeed, many of the services view parental involvement with suspicion. Although it is certainly important to safeguard the teen mother's right to make her own decision, this should not come at the expense of your right to proper counseling. If the authorities and counselors assisting your daughter do not appear sensitive to your concerns and worries, go elsewhere. Grandparenting support groups, clergy, and other professionals may be all of help.

Maintaining a Routine. No matter what you do, the nine months of pregnancy will be a period of turmoil and stress. It is crucial, therefore, that you do everything you can to help your daughter maintain some sort of stability in her life. For most teens, school and their contact with their school friends is the heart of their daily routine. It is hardly surprising that most counselors believe that it is important that the expectant mother continue to attend classes at her regular school. Although it was common in the past to expel pregnant students, *this is no longer legal in public schools.* It is also illegal to prevent teen mothers from attending school. Private schools are much more free to set their own policies on such issues. However, even if your daughter's school mandates her expulsion, you have little to lose by appealing to the administration. Often such rules remain on the books until the authorities are faced with an individual case that reminds them that teen mothers are not necessarily troublemakers and delinquents but may be good students, class leaders, and star athletes.

Whether you have a choice or not, you may want to look into the possibility of sending your daughter to a special school for pregnant teens. This may mean moving to another area for the duration of the pregnancy, but it has the advantage that your daughter will no longer be in the minority in her school. Her meetings with other girls in her situation, particularly those who have had their babies and are already parenting, may also open her eyes to the reality of single parenting and other issues.

Some pregnant teens and their families choose a maternity home as the best arrangement. Although such institutions still carry the stigma of the old "homes for wayward girls," most usually provide a warm and supportive environment. Some states also cover the fees for such residences.

Exploring the Adoption Option. Expectant teens and their parents rarely consider the possibility of adoption as a *first* resort. For many, it seems obvious that they must be the ones to raise their child/grandchild. But it's important to explore all options before you make a final decision. Counseling services are available in most communities to help you explore all the possibilities.

If you and your child decide that it is best to offer her child (your grandchild) for adoption, it may mean the end of any significant contact with or knowledge of your grandchild. In many cases you will not even know your grandchild's name. The process, except in the rarest of circumstances, is irreversible. Therefore, this is a decision that your child must consider seriously, with an awareness of all the consequences. The counseling service or adoption agency you consult will be able to offer you a detailed explanation of the adoption process. (I discussed the other side of this process, grandparenting an adopted child, in the previous chapter.)

In the past, adoption was often a rather impersonal affair in which birthparents and adoptive parents never met and had only limited knowledge of and access to each other. This approach, known as closed adoption, is still common in many areas. However, more and more birthparents, adoptive parents, and grandparents favor a more personal approach, in which they meet each other and remain in contact. Birthparents in particular prefer the option of an open adoption, in which they meet the adoptive parents and have continuing contact with them. In many cases, having seen with their own eyes that the baby is well cared for, they feel much more at peace.

In most states the father's signature is required for an adoption to become final. You must always remember that your daughter's child has two sets of birthgrandparents. The father's parents may wish to raise the child, and even if you are not pleased with this, you should consider it as a possibility. Moreover, they can (through their son) seriously impede your own efforts to put the child up for adoption.

After the Adoption

Although birthparents are frequently told, "You'll forget it; it will go away," erasing one of the most significant events in your life is a virtual impossibility. Indeed, if the testimonies gathered by Concerned United Birthparents (CUB), an organization of parents who have surrendered their children for adoption, is representative, most of them "cannot forget the most profound experience of our lives nor does the pain of losing our children diminish." So if adoption is the option your daughter chooses, do not expect her to move on quickly or easily. Allow her to grieve and to express her feelings of pain. The childless mother has not only physically carried her child throughout the pregnancy but often carries it with her mentally for many years to come. Birthdays and other dates that would have been significant milestones can be particularly difficult.

Even if you have been completely supportive of your daughter's decision to give up your grandchild for adoption, this doesn't necessarily mean that it will be emotionally easy for you. Sometimes it only hits you when you *don't* bring a grandchild home from the hospital or when a friend begins to talk about her grandchildren.

Although, in the past, closed adoptions meant that adopted children were deprived of any knowledge of or contact with their birthfamilies, this has changed. In recent years, adopted children have become far more aggressive about their rights to identify their birthparents. Thus, years after the event (usually when the surrendered child is an adult), your grandchild may reenter his mother's life and yours as well. Director Mike Leigh's recent movie *Secrets and Lies* provided a powerful depiction of how the reappearance of a child given up for adoption can affect the mother and her family.

Jeanne Warren Lindsay's *Parents, Pregnant Teens and the Adoption Option: Help for Families* (Morning Glory Press, 1989) is a useful guide to this subject. (For further information on adoption see the groups and sources listed at the end of this and the previous chapter.)

Teenage Fathers and the Paternal Grandparents

Thus far in this chapter, most of the information has been directed to the parents of the teen mother. But this is only one side of the story. While it may be your daughter who is carrying the baby, this child, like every other, has two birthparents. It is important, therefore, that before you go too far, you consider the role of the birthfather. Obviously, this is of even more immediate concern if the boy in question is your son.

The common stereotype of the teen father is that of a promiscuous, immature, semi-delinquent who is unwilling to take responsibility for either his own behavior or the fate of his child. Although some young fathers may fit this image, most do not. Most studies have indicated that adolescent fathers attend prenatal classes, provide at least some support to the expectant mother, and help out by providing transportation and running errands both before and after the baby is born. Yet even when the teen father wants to be involved with the pregnancy and the child, this is often not easy. The maternal grandparents, buying into the stereotype, may assume that he won't be around or may be so angry that they exclude him. Often, it is the mother-to-be who attempts to exclude him. All too often, social service agencies will go along with their wishes. Most programs for high school–age parents give little or no attention to the fathers. Even in those cases where there is no overt antagonism toward the father, he and his parents often get lost in the shuffle.

Probably the first thing you will have to do for your son, after you have had a good discussion and fully understand most of his concerns and wishes, is to act as his advocate. Do not let his confusion and uncertainty make him a mere bystander in the birth and life choices of his child, your grand-child. In many cases, the maternal grandparents and even the mother may be more willing to sit and discuss things with you than they are with him. Professionals have often found that group sessions with both sets of grandparents and the teen parents can go a long way in resolving conflicts and facilitating decision making.

In order to make the most of your involvement, you need to be clear about your own intentions. What role do you see yourselves, the paternal grandparents, playing? Unfortunately, the involvement of the paternal grandmother and grandfather has generally been more an exception than a norm. Yet it stands to reason that their active participation can serve not only to meet the emotional needs of the father but also to widen the potential support system for the adolescent mother and baby.

Even before your grandchild is born, there are a number of things you can do to prepare your son for fatherhood. These include seeing that he has access to accurate information on the pregnancy and birth process, encouraging him to be better informed and more responsible with regard to birth control, locating a teen parent or teen father program, and providing the conditions necessary for him to continue his education or occupational training so that he can he can properly provide for his child.

In short, whether you are the paternal or maternal grandparents, I would encourage you to push for the active involvement of both parents in the pregnancy, childbirth, and all other decisions concerning your grandchild. Precisely what form this involvement takes will vary from case to case, but there is nothing to be gained for either side by excluding teen fathers.

Teen Marriage

In years gone by, it was usually expected that if a girl got pregnant, the man or boy responsible would do "the honorable thing" and marry her. No one knows how many children were born "early" to couples who married after discovering they were expecting a child. This was the case with my own parents.

Today, as the high rates of single-parent families testify, this is no longer the case. The divorce rate for teenagers under eighteen who marry because of pregnancy is four times that of couples in their twenties. Under the best of circumstances, teen couples find life difficult and are often unprepared for their passage into adulthood. If their transition is even more sudden and is further complicated by a pregnancy and the need to care for an infant the risk of divorce is even greater.

Put in other terms, the vast majority of teens who marry because of a pregnancy end up divorcing. Under these circumstances, marriage is at best a risky solution—if it is a solution at all. Teen mothers often find that when they marry, they have responsibility not only for a child but also for a household, including a husband who expects them to take sole or primary responsibility for cooking, cleaning, shopping, and child care. Teen fathers often have great difficulty dealing with normal adolescent issues and parenthood at the same time.

Since young parents are usually short on time and money, the expectations they have of you as a grandparent may not be very different from those of your single teen mother. They may assume that they can count on your support and even expect to live with you. It is a good idea to discuss all of this with them as the plans for marriage are pieced together.

The Three-Generation Household

In contrast to the preceding options, raising your grandchild, whether by yourself or with one or both of her parents, carries with it both immediate and long-term implications.

You can raise your grandchild yourself, at least until the mother is better prepared to do so herself. I discuss the many issues and options that arise in this situation in Chapter 12.

If you are considering raising your grandchild along with your son or daughter, there are a number of practical questions you need to keep in mind. Do you have the room and the financial resources? How will you provide medical insurance and medical care for your grandchild? How will the presence of a baby (nephew or niece) and a young parent affect your other children who still live at home?

Remember that it is a good idea to work out as many ground rules as possible *before* the new parent and grandchild are settled in. In particular, you need to be clear about what financial support and/or other kinds of help (baby-sitting, day care, transportation) you will be expected to provide. Are you expecting your child to go back to school or to find work? Jeanne Warren Lindsay's *School-Age Parents: The Challenge of Three-Generation Living* (Morning Glory Press, 1990) is an excellent guide for grandparents that I warmly recommend.

Adult Single Mothers: Then Comes Marriage?

Over the past quarter-century, as the median age of marriage has risen, so has the percentage of people who never marry. From 1970 to 1997, the number of people who had never married more than doubled from 21.4 million to 45.8 million. In fact, never-married persons (as opposed to divorced or widowed persons) today account for the largest number of unmarried adults.

Although in the past those who did not marry usually decided not to have children, this is no longer the case. In the previous section, I noted the rise in births to unmarried women during the past quarter-century and emphasized the phenomenon of teen pregnancies. Teen pregnancies are only a very small part of this story, however. In 1970, only 31,000 babies were born to unmarried women over age thirty; by 1992, this number had risen to 191,000! (Almost a third, 63,000, were over thirty-five years of age.) Although some of these are children born to women who *also* had babies at a younger age, an increasing number are cases of what one author has called "motherhood by conviction." Women in their thirties and early forties who wish to have children before their biological clock runs down but have not found or don't wish to be with a husband are increasingly having babies. (For a discussion of lesbian mothers, see Chapter 9.) While many are adopting children, others are bearing biological children of their own through artificial insemination.

Many of the issues that arise when your teenage child has a baby are not relevant when your thirty-something daughter becomes a mother. (Single men are also, but less frequently, adopting children.) In many cases of older single mothers, it is a conscious decision rather than a failure of contraception that leads to pregnancy and motherhood. Many older singles have deferred motherhood in order to pursue their careers and thus are economically fairly well off or at least professionally secure. Among the celebrities who have pursued this route in recent years are Madonna and Jodie Foster.

Despite these well-known examples and the general rise in the number of mothers by conviction, it is still a comparative rarity, and they make up only a small percentage of the millions of women who never marry in the United States. This is no doubt due to the stigma that still attaches to "illegitimate" births and the logistical problems that caring for a child pose for any single parent, regardless of age or financial standing. In some European countries, many of the practical difficulties remain. Despite generous government policies, single parents are still twice as likely as the rest of the population to be poor. But the stigma has all but vanished, and the data are remarkably different. In Norway, Sweden, and Denmark, for example, almost half of all children are born outside of marriage, many to women in their twenties and thirties who have decided not to marry.

Although an older child may not need the same kind of support that a younger single mother needs, she may still need lots of help from you. At the least, she will want your support and understanding for her decision. More practically, she may need help with logistics, such as child care when she is at work, baby-sitting when she wants to go out, and various types of pinch-hitting if she's ill or otherwise disposed.

Further Reading and Resources

ALEXANDER, SHOSHANA. *In Praise of Single Parents: Mothers and Fathers Embracing the Challenge* (Boston: Houghton Mifflin, 1996).

ARTHUR, SHIRLEY. *Surviving Teen Pregnancy: Your Choices, Dreams & Decisions* (Buena Park, CA: Morning Glory Press, 1991).

BUCKINGHAM, ROBERT W., and MARY P. DERBY. *"I'm Pregnant, Now What Do I Do?"* (Amherst, NY: Prometheus Books, 1997).

COLES, ROBERT, with ROBERT E. COLES, DANIEL A. COLES and MICHAEL H. COLES. *The Youngest Parents: Teen Pregnancy as It Shapes Lives* (New York: W.W. Norton, 1997). Photographs by Jocelyn Lee and John Moses.

LINDSAY, JEANNE WARREN. *Parents, Pregnant Teens and the Adoption Option: Help for Families* (Buena Park, CA: Morning Glory Press, 1989).

————. *School-Age Parents: The Challenge of Three-Generation Living* (Buena Park, CA: Morning Glory Press, 1990).

National Organization of Single Mothers
P.O. Box 68
Midland, NC 28107-0068
704-888-5063
Provides practical information for single mothers (and fathers), with an emphasis on self-help and support groups. Publishes *Single Mother.* Call 704-888-KIDS for a free back issue.

One Parent Families Association of Canada
6979 Yonge Street
Suite 203
Willowdale, Ontario
M2M 3X9
416-226-0062
oneparent@titan.tcn.net

Parents Without Partners
401 North Michigan Ave
Chicago, IL 60611
312-644-6610
Local chapters across the United States. Also publishes *Single Parent* magazine.

ROBINSON, BRYAN. *Teenage Fathers* (Lexington, MA: Lexington Books, 1988).

Single Mothers by Choice
P.O. Box 1642 Gracie Square Station
New York, NY 10028
212-988-0993
Provides information (publishing a newsletter), support, and resources for women who choose to be single mothers. Support groups exist in many locales.

www.single-fathers.org

11

Until Divorce Do Us Part

In 1986, Andrew J. Cherlin and Frank F. Furstenburg published their study, *The New American Grandparent*. The book was then and still is in many ways a landmark in the study of grandparents in the United States. It was one of the first works to call attention to the fact that divorce affects not only children and parents but also grandparents. The title they chose for their chapter on this subject, "A Special Case: Grandparents and Divorce," appears rather surprising, especially considering that only five years later, the same two authors would collaborate in writing *Divided Families: What Happens to Children When Parents Part*.

Far from being a special case, divorce has been a common feature of American family life since at least the 1960s. And although Americans are more likely to divorce than any other people, Western Europeans have closed the gap in the past two decades. Even in Japan there are at present 24 divorces for every 100 marriages. Over half of all marriages in the United States end in divorce. Many of these are what the *New York Times* called "starter marriages"—brief, childless unions of one or two years. Nevertheless, every year, one million children (somebody's grandchildren) experience their parents' divorce.

Even the most amicable of breakups can take a heavy toll on children. No matter how often parents try to explain that their divorce has nothing to do with their feelings about their children ("We'll both always love you") how could kids not feel some combination of rejection and guilt when their parents tell them they're splitting up? ("If I had been a better girl and obeyed more often, Mommy and Daddy would still be together.")

Judith Wallerstein, an expert in the field, wrote in her 1980 book, *Surviving the Breakup: How Children and Parents Cope with Divorce:* "Children often feel abandoned or rejected by the parent who leaves the family home: younger children, especially, experience it as evidence of their own lack of worth. This blow to pride and self-esteem provokes anger in many children of divorce."

Compared to the population at large, adolescent children of divorced parents are less likely to graduate from high school, tend to marry at an earlier age, have a lower probability of ever marrying, and if they do, are more likely eventually to be divorced themselves.

All of this might seem like an argument for trying to convince your adult children to remain married at all costs. This is not my opinion. All studies of and statements about the negative effects of divorce have a central problem: Because there is no control group, it is *impossible* to tell what the effects on the children would have been if their parents had stayed together ("for the sake of the children") in their unhappy marriage. In other words, comparing children of divorce with the general population is statistically fallacious, because the divorced group is self-selected. It consists of couples with problems so great that they eventually decided to divorce. If anybody can find a group of couples with problems of equal magnitude who didn't divorce, *then* we will have some truly valuable studies.

There is no doubt that living in a home with continual stress and conflict, regardless of how many parents are present, is hardly beneficial for a child. One recent poll found that people whose parents had divorced were significantly more likely than people whose parents had "happy" marriages to agree with the statement, "When parents continually fight, children are better off if the parents divorce."

Another study looked at the self-esteem of children in different family structures. *When poverty was removed as a factor,* there was no difference among the structures. The children with the lowest self-esteem came from intact two-parent families in which the parents had a low level of interest.

As Cherlin and Furstenberg note, "Divorce is not a good thing for children. . . . But it's not as consistent a negative effect as some people claim. Most people who have studied the subject believe it's better to grow up with one loving parent than two fighting parents."

Some Harsh Economic Truths

There is one incontrovertible negative effect of divorce: economics. One study found that women experience a 73 percent *drop* in the standard of living after a divorce, while men experience a 42 percent *improvement.* Throw into the mix the fact that women most often have custody of the child or children, the trend away from alimony payments, the fact that women consistently earn lower salaries than men, even when performing the same jobs, and the well-documented failures of men to pay child support, and you have a recipe for disaster. More than 25 percent of women (and their children, if any) fall into poverty at some point in the first five years after divorce. Divorced black women and their children are especially vulnerable. A 1988 study found that more than 61 percent of them lived in poverty.

Although I never felt myself to be in the dire straits faced by some of these women, I am familiar with their predicament. Following my divorce from Miriam's father, Dan, the biggest challenge we faced was economic. I had a job doing market research, calling people up on the phone and asking their opinions about one thing or another. I was paid one dollar an hour. From this I had to pay our $75 a month rent, clothe us, and feed us. I'm still not sure how I did it. We led Spartan lives. I *never* bought new clothes.

Miriam received a lot of love from me and my wonderful group of friends. But I wonder, if I had not remarried, how high a standard of living I would have been able to provide for her and whether she would have been able to go to the best schools and live in a household where finances were not a constant concern, and I wonder what effect these uncertainties would have had on her.

An organization called Jewish Family Service paid for Miriam to stay with a foster family during the day while I went to work and twice a week to classes at the New School for Social Research. The family lived about ten blocks from our house, and I would wheel her there in the morning and pick her up at night, which was not easy in the rain, snow, and ice. The family would feed her, but when I picked her up I hadn't eaten, and I will always remember how hungry I was. When she was three, Jewish Family Service paid for her to go to a German Jewish Orthodox nursery school, which was wonderful. The people loved her—they were like grandparents to her—and it was a wonderful atmosphere for Miriam. Not everyone is so fortunate to have such a fine support system. Even if you can't help your grandchildren directly, you may be able to assist in locating services similar to those that were so important to Miriam and me during our time of need.

Breaking Up Is Hard to Do

Despite the fact that divorce is so common, everyone seems to believe it can't happen in their family—*until it happens*. It always seems to come as a shock. All of us have known couples who seemed to be happily married, up until the day they announced their separation or divorce. All couples have problems, and sometimes those who seem to argue the loudest and the most frequently stay together the longest. Whatever the reasons, many parents report that they had no prior warning of the breakup of their adult child's marriage.

Short of a death, there is probably no event that disrupts family life as much as a divorce. Indeed, Joan Schrager Cohen, author of the excellent *Helping Your Grandchildren Through Their Parent's Divorce*, reports that many grandparents experience a period of mourning similar to that of the loss of a parent or spouse when their children divorce. Others find themselves suddenly reexamining their own marriage in the light of their children's decision. Although divorce by no means carries with it the stigma it held only a few decade ago, you may also feel a certain shame: "How can this happen in *our* family?" You should by no means deny these feelings. Share them with your friends or a personal counselor. But remember, however bad you may feel and however hard it is to tell your friends, the breakup of your child's marriage and your grandchildren's family is not primarily *your* story. There are lots of people you can share your feelings with, but your children and grandchildren need your support. Neither telling them how upset and disappointed you are nor providing a scorecard of the rights and wrongs of the different parties is going to help the situation.

Proceed with Caution

No matter how settled you may feel in your grandparenting style and in your relationship with your children and grandchildren, these will probably be thrown into turmoil by your children's divorce. If your child does not have custody of the children, you may find that you see them far less frequently and, in some cases, may even be totally denied access to them. On the other hand, if your child is the custodial parent and is caring for your grandchildren more or less on her own, you may be called upon to fill a much more instrumental role, providing far more practical support than in the past. Indeed, you may find many of the fun aspects of being a grandparent are overshadowed by daily demands for immediate assistance.

Before I talk about some of the things that you can do to help out, let me sound a note of caution. If you have always been an involved, take-charge type of person, your first inclination may be to move in (either physically or emotionally) and try to take care of everything. But hopping into your car or on the first plane in order to get things under control can easily be interpreted as a lack of confidence in your child's abilities. Always try to help your child handle the problems and challenges with your support, *before* you try and do it yourself. It is all too easy to find yourself cooking, cleaning, and caring for your adult child and grandchildren because of the crisis. Not only are they often too dazed to refuse the help you offer, but getting over-involved may well fill your need to do *something* in a situation that is really out of your control.

Although every family is different, most authorities agree you should be very careful about becoming too involved too quickly. Too much help can be just as harmful as not enough. Just because your child's marriage is over doesn't mean he has stopped being an adult. Always keep in mind that your primary goal throughout all the stages of your child's divorce is *to help him continue to function as an adult and as a parent.* Do not overwhelm him with lots of advice and instructions. One of the most important things you can do is provide emotional support while expressing your confidence in your child's ability to deal with the challenges and difficulties ahead. Remind him of other crises he has successfully weathered and the coping techniques that helped in those situations.

Do not interpret my advice to be cautious as an invitation to pull back and ignore the situation. There is nothing to be gained by denying this new reality. The trick is to find the right combination of emotional support and practical assistance.

When Steve and I were studying the families of Ethiopian Jews in Israel, we noted their high rate of divorce—several times the rate found among other Israelis (though not higher than that found here in the United States). Although we can't be sure, there is very little evidence that this rate was actually higher than what they experienced in Ethiopia. What was strikingly different were the consequences of the divorces. In Ethiopia, where extended families and large households dominated, children whose parents divorced may have found themselves in one-parent families but not one-*adult* families. Regardless of their parent's (usually the mother's) situation they found themselves surrounded by lots of other adults: aunts, uncles, older brothers or sisters, and of course grandparents. This traditional environment may contain some important lessons for us today. In America, the rise in divorce has largely coincided with the idealization of the nuclear family. Couples who divorce often find it difficult to take advantage of the support available in their extended family. I know we can't magically create extended families to help those who divorce, but grandparents have a vital role to play when their adult children divorce. This is especially true of grandfathers, since so many of the one-parent families that are created by divorce have no male figure present.

Helping with the Finances

When parents divorce, grandparents (especially if their child has custody) are frequently called upon to increase the practical support that they provide. Often this means helping out financially. Before you rush in, take a careful look at your financial picture, and be realistic about what commitments you can make in both the short and long term. Many experts recommend that before you discuss any details with your son or daughter, you should meet with an accountant or other financial expert to get a clear picture of your ability to help. Often an immediate infusion of money will be needed during the early stages to cover the expenses of your son's relocation or to tide your daughter over until child-care payments begin or she finds a new job. In the longer run, you may decide to assist with a particular expense, such as mortgage payments, rent, day care, or summer camp. In any event, it is important to set clear limits regarding the amount of money you can provide, for what purposes (job training, education, mortgage payments), and over how much time.

Remember that even if you are quite well off and able to provide for your child and grandchildren for an extended period, this is not in either your or their best interest. Overdependence (like familiarity) breeds contempt, and however comfortable an adult child may be living off you, he will grow to resent it. Of course, if you lack the financial resources to help out but live close by, you may be able to help out by assisting with baby-sitting, carpooling, and generally increasing your involvement with your grandchildren.

In addition to considering your children's and grandchildren's immediate needs, you also need to consider the long-term implications of the divorce. Have your family lawyer look at your will and advise you about what changes need to be made to ensure that whatever you leave to posterity will stay in your family. Unfortunately, in most instances there is little you can do about past gifts, including family heirlooms and loans. But sound legal advice should ensure that your grandchildren's future interests are protected.

Can You Go Home Again?

Your adult child may wish to move back home, either with or without her children. According to the U.S. Census Bureau, in 1996 over 2 million children were living in their grandparents' home with one parent (in almost 90 percent of cases, their mother). This is never an ideal situation; it will undoubtedly disrupt your routine and, if they are still living at home, that of your other children. It also carries the danger of infantilizing your adult child and conveying the message that she is incapable of handling her own life just when her confidence is at its lowest. Whenever possible, adult children should be encouraged to maintain their independence and autonomy. Financial realities being what they are, however, moving back home may be the only viable short-term solution. If this appears to be the situation, you should agree on a clear set of house rules *before* your child and grandchildren have moved in.

Among the most important issues to be discussed regarding your adult child are curfews, household chores, sharing of finances, drinking, smoking, television, music, and overnight guests. Discussing such details in advance drives home the reality of moving back home. Many adult children decide *not* to move back home when they fully understand what it entails. Although this may sound cold or heartless, it is preferable to plunging everyone's daily life into turmoil with constant quarrels.

With regard to your grandchildren, you and their parent should agree in advance about your child-care responsibilities, especially discipline. In Chapter 12, I discuss the topic of grandparents as parents in some detail. In some ways, having total responsibility for your grandchildren is easier than suddenly having them in your house and having to work out a shared arrangement.

Custodial Fathers

Thus far, I have been operating, perhaps a bit unfairly, under the assumption that the mother, your daughter, has primary responsibility for your grandchildren after the divorce. Although the number of custodial fathers in the United States is rising far faster (from just over 1 million in 1980 to over 2.7 million in 1996) than the number of single mothers, they are still a relatively small percentage (about 14 percent) of single-parent families. Nonetheless, the number of dads choosing the daddy track will probably only grow, and it is important to acknowledge some of the special issues that you may face if your son has custody of your grandchildren.

Although it is commonly assumed that fathers who are awarded custody (or joint custody) are better prepared to care for children than their noncustodial counterparts, there is little evidence to support this assumption. Research on custodial fathers has tended to show that they were not especially involved in either child care or housework *prior* to their divorce. In the words of Geoffrey L. Grief, author of *The Daddy Track and the Single Father,* single fathers, "are not extraordinary men who have had extraordinary childhoods or marriages . . . they do not bring any particular expertise to the many tasks of single parenting they face. As such, their successes are even more gratifying and encouraging, because they show that with little previous training men can adapt to raising their children alone."

What this means on a practical level is that in addition to all the other adjustments your son (or son-in-law) will find himself making, he is probably going to have to learn a lot more than ever before about running a household: cooking, cleaning, laundry, and so on. Who can forget the marvelous scene in the Academy Award–winning film *Kramer vs. Kramer* in which Dustin Hoffman struggles to prepare French toast the first morning after his wife's departure? (Or the ease with which he accomplishes the same task several months later?) If your son is like most, during the early period as a single parent, he's going to need a lot of support and assistance as he learns to be a housekeeper.

It is not a good idea to rush in too quickly. Wait to be invited. Although you probably have a good idea of which household skills your son has and which he lacks, several years of living on his own and of married life may have widened his repertoire. Most single fathers report that the first few months of housekeeping were the most difficult. As he settles into a household routine, your son will probably welcome the household tips you share and will be particularly interested in how you make those special foods that his children seem to like.

Keep in mind that every housekeeper has his or her particular style and priorities. And do not expect a single parent of either gender to have the time or energy to meet the most exacting standards of cleaning and cooking. Even if the sheets aren't laundered as often as you think they should be or the rug isn't vacuumed to your liking, the important thing is that your grandchildren are being cared for in a safe and stable home environment.

The practical aspects of housekeeping are only a small part of the story for single fathers. Unfortunately, there are no simple recipes or shortcuts for dealing with the emotional upheaval of the situation. As I noted earlier, many custodial fathers have surprisingly little experience dealing with their children's emotional life. Needless to say, the turmoil of divorce is hardly the ideal situation in which to begin such an undertaking. Many men still carry with them the idea that there is something "unmanly" about nurturing and physical affection.

Encourage your son to love his children unconditionally— to hug them, hold them, and say how much he loves them. Help him to believe in himself as a parent and to trust his instincts and feelings. Reach out to him and your grandchildren, and let them know how proud they make you. In the long run, many fathers take deep satisfaction in the relationships they forge with their children following their divorce.

It is not surprising that raising a teenage daughter is one of the biggest challenges faced by many single fathers. I vividly remember listening to a young African-American woman on a television talk show recounting her father's attempts to raise her alone. Her laughter mixed with tears as she told of his attempts to fix her hair, buy her the right clothes, and be both mother and father to her.

If your granddaughter's mother is still in the picture, it would be best for all concerned that she be as involved as possible. However, grandmothers often have a special role to play when the discussion turns to "girl talk," whether it be questions about puberty and adolescence or practical tips on hygiene, clothes, makeup, and hairstyling. In many cases, your granddaughter's father will probably give a sigh of relief when you offer to step in and assist in buying her first bra or helping pick out a special dress for a party. But if he resists or feels that your intervention is in some way a criticism of his parenting, don't be offended. Try to help him understand that your involvement reflects your desire to share special moments with your granddaughter, not an attempt to deprive or criticize him. Whatever you do, don't place your granddaughter in an impossible situation by saying, "Let her decide." Being asked to choose between you and her father is unfair to her and to both of you.

One other word about teenage granddaughters and custodial fathers: It is reasonable for children, especially teens, to have chores and to help out around the house. As a rule, such matters are best left to be decided between parent and child, even if you feel that one of your grandchildren is shouldering more than his or her fair share of responsibility. However, it is a good idea to keep a special eye on the role of older girls. Although it is completely natural for older children to pitch in and share in the shopping, cooking, and cleaning, they should not be expected or encouraged to substitute for their (absent) mothers as housekeepers. Even if your granddaughter professes to enjoy taking care of the family, do your best to encourage her father to let her be a normal teenager.

Talking to Your Grandchild

Unless your grandchildren are still infants, you will probably find yourself talking to them about their parents' divorce. Remember that this is an opportunity to provide love, support, and stability, not to vent your feelings or present your side of the breakup. Although it will not always be easy, you must make every effort to remain neutral when discussing events. Whatever problems you may have had in the past with your child or her spouse, this is not the time or place to rehash them. Nor should you be the source for details on the reasons for or the progress of their parents' divorce.

Your grandchildren, especially the younger ones, may be feeling as if their whole world was falling apart. Reassure them that you love them.

Many of the questions I have been asked as Dr. Ruth, psychosexual therapist, have begun, "I have a friend who . . .". Although it is always tempting to reply, "Well, tell your friend to call me and then we can talk about it," I've come to understand that many people need to distance themselves from their questions to cover their embarrassment about sexual matters. This sort of distancing (professionals usually refer to it as displacement) can be a valuable technique when talking to your grandchildren about their feelings concerning their parents' divorce. Although they are probably feeling more pain, guilt, and anger than embarrassment, it is still a useful tool. Rather than asking directly how your grandson feels about his situation, you can lead into the topic by noting, "A book I read said that many children feel guilty about their parents' separation" or "A friend of mine said that her grandson had trouble concentrating in school after his father moved out." Although this doesn't always immediately kick off a conversation, eventually it usually works.

This can also be a good way to convey valuable information that may cut through the isolation your grandchild may be feeling. Despite the fact that divorce is so common, many children (as well as parents and grandparents) feel abandoned and alone with their feelings when it happens to them. Remind them that lots of children you know or have read about have been through similar experiences. (Without, of course, denying the reality of their special pain.) This is also a good technique for reassuring your grandchild that regardless of who he lives with—you, his mother, his father, or in a blended family—families are not necessarily two biological parents and their children.

Visitation

So far I have been talking about those grandparents who are able to maintain contact with their grandchildren. A whole different set of challenges appear when grandparents are denied the right to see their grandchildren. This usually happens to the parents of the noncustodial parent, especially when the divorce has been particularly bitter.

Cherlin and Furstenberg write, "If your daughter's marriage breaks up, your relationship with your grandchildren will probably be maintained or even enhanced; but if your son's marriage breaks up, your relationship with your grandchildren is likely to be diminished in quantity and probably in quality as well." When they were writing it was almost always the mother who got custody, and although this has changed somewhat and joint custody is also more common, paternal grandparents are still usually the ones who suffer.

If you have had a good relationship with your daughter-in-law or son-in-law and the other grandparents in the past, it will help keep them from turning you into an "out-law." The better your lines of communication, the easier it will be to explain that the grandparent-grandchild bond is too important to be severed or held hostage to a middle-generation breakup. Remember that everyone will be hurting and in a process of recovery, so don't make too many demands too soon. Short-term difficulties may be resolved with time.

If you have exhausted your patience and are still denied

access to your grandchildren, consider your options and your rights. Before pursuing a legal remedy, explore the possibility of mediation by a family friend, a relative, or a professional. If you have built a strong relationship with the other grandparents, they may be willing and able to use their influence to reunite you with your grandchildren. You may find that the services of a professional family mediator are more effective. Such experts, found in most Yellow Pages, are professionally trained to assist families in resolving disputes without recourse to the courts. Not only are they usually more effective than most amateurs (however well intentioned), but they are cheaper and less confrontational than legal remedies.

In some cases, there may be no alternative but to turn to the courts. Since the mid-1970s, grandparents' visitation rights have been debated in state legislatures across the country. It is a testimony to the effectiveness of grandparents' rights organizations that today nearly all states have laws allowing grandparents to petition courts to continue seeing their grandchildren in the event of divorce or death of a child's parents. Note, however, that this is not a guarantee of visitation rights but of the right to petition. Most states have a variety of criteria that are used in determining the best interest of the child. Your local or state grandparents' group can probably fill you in on the situation in your state. Most authorities advise grandparents to consult a specialist in family law before proceeding too far. Such specialized legal assistance is vital if you decide to pursue your cause in court. Visitation cases, whether they involve parents or grandparents, can be incredibly messy and complicated, so it's always best to have an expert advocate at your side.

Remarriage and Stepgrandchildren

Not only does the United States have the world's highest divorce rate, it also has the highest percentage of remarriages. Almost three-quarters of divorced men and about three-fifths of divorced women eventually acquire a new spouse, and the majority of children of single parents in time acquire a stepparent and stepgrandparents. Every day 1,300 couples with children remarry. In the United States today, almost 10 million children under age eighteen live in "blended" (this term is usually used to replace "step") families. According to one estimate, 35 percent of all children born in the early 1980s will spend part of their childhoods living in such households.

Thus, the divorce-remarriage cycle has created millions of new stepfamilies. If your child's divorce has resulted in a much deeper involvement in her life and those of your grandchildren, remarriage may require you to pull back once again. In some respects, this may be welcome. In most cases, entering into a new marriage means a significant economic improvement for mother and children. It also has other benefits. Stepparents get a bad rap in fairy tales and other literature, and no one would claim that second marriages are conflict-free, but a stepparent is, if nothing else, another pair of hands. You will probably be relieved of some of the responsibilities you had prior to the remarriage.

Although you may welcome the chance to go back to being just a grandparent, letting go again may not be so easy, and you may not want to give up all that extra time with your grandchildren. You will acquire a new set of in-laws as well. If your new son-in-law has no children of his own, the adjustment in your relationship with your grandchildren may be comparatively minor. If, on the other hand, your new son-in-law or daughter-in-law has children from a previous marriage, you will have acquired instant stepgrandchildren. That is what happened to the Huxtables in "The Cosby Show" when their daughter Denise married a man with a child from a previous marriage.

If your child marries someone with children before she has any of her own, your *first* experience with grandchildren may be with stepgrandchildren. That was the situation for Fred's parents. When Fred and I married, Miriam became their first (step) grandchild and they became her only (step) grandparents. I had always regretted that she had no grandparents. (Her father Dan's parents had never been part of her life.) Fred's parents met Miriam for the first time at our wedding, and I still remember the instant bond that was forged between her and Fred's father.

Although "The Brady Bunch" was probably the first television show to present a blended family (and the blending here resulted from death rather than divorce), its portrayal was so idealized as to make it a sort of blended "Leave It to Beaver." In reality, despite their apparent ubiquity, society at large doesn't make things very easy for such families. Stepparents usually have to deal with a wide array of obstacles that are individually minor but collectively infuriating. Many of these are symptomatic of the prevailing narrow definitions of family and will thus be familiar to you as grandparents if you have ever had to care for your grandchildren for any length of time. A doctor might refuse to discuss a child's medical condition with a stepparent, a day-care center might not let a stepparent pick up a child, or an insurance package might not cover stepchildren.

Only a fraction of the tensions and ambivalences faced by blended families are the product of outside forces, however. This new situation is a big adjustment for everyone. The parents will be adjusting to the intricacies of their new household. Sharing a house and finances and raising children together are all learning experiences. Your new daughter-in-law will probably feel tremendous pressure to keep from being cast as the evil stepmother to your grandchildren. Most experts agree that it takes anywhere from two to five years for blended families to settle into a more or less comfortable regime.

One thing you must always keep in mind: Your child's remarriage doesn't mean that your grandchildren no longer need you. It simply means yet another shift in your role. In many cases, while the daily practical assistance you are required to provide diminishes, your role as confidant or model comes to the fore. Most children find the presence of a new adult in the house disruptive, especially if they have harbored hopes—against all odds—that their parents would get back together again. They probably won't feel comfortable voicing this to their mother or father, so you may be called upon to provide a shoulder to cry on. It is important that you assure them that one parent's decision to remarry is neither a betrayal of the other nor a threat to their own position. In a similar fashion, by showing an open mind and a willingness to accept your new son-in-law or daughter-in-law, you can provide your grandchildren with a model of cordial family relations in a time of change.

You and Your Stepgrandchildren

The type of relationship you develop with your stepgrandchild will depend on a number of variables. First and foremost, there is the relationship of your adult child (the stepparent) with her new stepchild. This is not to suggest that you can't develop a relationship that is in some way independent, but there are some practical considerations. If your child is not married to the custodial parent or if the stepchildren are in college or are young adults out on their own, you may not have many opportunities to develop a relationship. If your stepgrandchildren already have grandparents (as many as four), they may not particularly feel a need to add grandparents number five and six.

The age of your stepgrandchildren at the time when you enter their lives is also of major importance. In general, children who are ten or older have a harder time making the adjustment to the new family situation than younger children do. Teens can find it a particularly difficult adjustment. Although infants, toddlers, and small children may accept you into their lives naturally, older children may not be so open to the change.

Whatever your feelings, don't rush into things. Children have very good "BS detectors," so don't overwhelm them by acting the way you think you should or forcing the feelings if they're not there. Read up on stepfamilies and be patient until you see how you can most effectively help your family. Don't feel that there is something wrong if you don't immediately click with your stepgrandchild. In stepgrandparenting, as in so much of life, timing is crucial.

Remember that love is not a limited resource. Neither you nor your grandchildren will have less to give if you care for your stepgrandchildren. Instead of trying to achieve the same relationship with your stepgrandchild as with your grandchild, focus on achieving the best relationship you can. As we saw already in our discussion of grandchildren, it is impossible to treat children identically. And treating them equally does not mean keeping score. This is also true with regard to your new stepgrandchildren. It is much more important to get to know each of your grandchildren as an individual than to give each of them exactly the same gift.

You may be convinced that you will never be able to really care for a child with whom you share neither blood ties nor a genetic connection. This is more a cultural assumption than an immutable truth. In modern America and in many other societies, it is often assumed that blood ties are the only real basis of family. As I have already discussed in the chapter on families, adoption, artificial fertilization, and other forms of family show that this is a misconception.

When Grandparents Divorce

Divorces, remarriages, blended families, and stepchildren do not suddenly disappear with time; they simply evolve into the next stages of the family cycle. Stepchildren grow up, marry, and have children of their own. Divorced parents and stepparents become grandparents. One result of the high divorce rate since the 1960s is that grandchildren are frequently born into complex family situations with several sets of grandparents and stepgrandparents.

In addition, many more couples decide to get divorced after their kids are grown or even after their grandchildren are born. Many of the rules that I mentioned concerning your children's divorce apply to your own divorce as well. In particular, you must avoid putting your children and grandchildren in the middle. There is nothing to be gained by badmouthing your spouse or creating unnecessary conflicts. Holidays and other family events will be hard enough for everyone whatever you do. If you tell your children that you won't attend your grandchild's christening, bar mitzvah, or wedding if your former spouse attends, you have created a no-win situation. Even if they don't invite the other grandparent, the absence will be blamed on you.

Although a grandparent's divorce is usually less traumatic than a parent's, your grandchildren will need to be reassured that your breakup has nothing to do with them. If you were a major stabilizer during other family crises, your divorce may be particularly unsettling.

Get a life! You can certainly turn to your family for support and understanding, but don't be a burden. Throwing yourself headlong into *their* lives won't solve *your* problems. Maybe your husband never liked opera, but you really like opera, so find somebody to go to the opera with you. Maybe you want to start gardening or go to community college. Take some adult education courses. If you just wallow in grief and feel sorry for yourself, you will not form new friendships; and I'm not necessarily talking about new romantic relationships, just people who want to be with you.

Whether its yours or your children's, divorce is one of the toughest experiences any family can go through. And though it hasn't yet become as inevitable as death and taxes, it is a lot more common than in the past. No matter what you do, it will never be easy. But with careful thought and wise action, you can perhaps minimize the toll it exacts from your grandchildren.

Further Reading and Resources

ATKINSON, CHRISTINE. *Step-Parenting: Understanding the Emotional Problems and Stresses* (Rochester, VT: Thorsons Publishing, 1986).

COHEN, JOAN SCHRAGER. *Helping Your Grandchildren Through Their Parents' Divorce* (New York: Walker and Company, 1994).

Divorcenet: Family Law Advisor Grandparent Issues Message Board
www.divorcenet.com
This website deals with all aspects of divorce. Under Grandparent Issues, there are chat forums and access to resource pages from 17 states and the District of Columbia.

EINSTEIN, ELIZABETH. *The Stepfamily: Living, Loving & Learning* (Boston: Shambhala, 1985).

Full-Time Dads: The Journal for Caring Fathers
P.O. Box 577
Cumberland, ME 04021
207-829-5260

GOTTLIEB, DOROTHY WEISS, INEZ BELLOW GOTTLIEB, and MAJORIE A. SLAVIN. *What to Do When Your Son or Daughter Divorces* (New York: Bantam Books, 1988), especially Chapter 8, "There's No Such Thing as an Ex-Grandparent."

GRIEF, GEOFFREY L. *The Daddy Track and the Single Father* (Lexington, MA: Lexington Books, 1990).

JOHNSON, COLLEEN LEAHY. *Ex Familia: Grandparents, Parents and Children Adjust to Divorce* (New Brunswick, NJ: Rutgers University Press, 1988).

KELLEY, PATRICIA. *Developing Healthy Stepfamilies: Twenty Families Tell Their Stories.* (New York: The Haworth Press, 1990).

Mothers without Custody
P.O. Box 27418
Houston, TX 77227
800-457-6962

National Council of Children's Rights
Strengthening Families and Assisting Children of Separation and Divorce
220 I. Street N.W.
Suite 230
Washington, DC 20002
202-547-NCCR

12

Starting Over: Grandparents as Parents

Ellen was only eight years old when her father became ill. She was sent to live with her paternal grandparents. She stayed for a year, through her father's final illness and death. Her grandfather taught her to play chess. After her father's death, she went back to live with her mother, but the memory of her year with her grandparents always stayed with her.

Ray, a forty-two-year-old African-American woman, is by any standards an extraordinarily giving woman. In addition to raising four children of her own, she has an adopted daughter, the child of a friend, who has been in and out of prison and on and off drugs. Countless other children have lived in Ray's house, some for only a few days and others for weeks, months, or even longer. It was therefore only natural that when her daughter called from college to tell her she was pregnant, Ray agreed to be responsible for her grandchild, at least until graduation. Still, money is always short. And sometimes Ray says, "I've been taking care of children for twenty-four years. . . . Sometimes I get so tired of it."

Unplanned Parenthood

Sometimes it comes about gradually, as the culmination of a series of (usually tragic) events. And sometimes there is no warning: a phone call in the middle of the night or a social worker appearing at the door. At first you may be asked to take care of your grandchild for a few days; then the periods get longer. One day you realize that you're not just baby-sitting anymore. Whatever the circumstances, more and more grandparents find themselves caring for their grandchildren full time.

While some authors romanticize these second-time parents and point to a long tradition of grandparents helping to raise children, most third-generation caregivers agree there is very little that is "grand" about becoming parents yet again. The children they care for are more often than not victims of the five *D*s: drugs, death, disease, divorce, and desertion. Incarceration, teen pregnancy, and child abuse also contribute their share. Put rather simply, grandparents raise their grandchildren because their grandchildren need someone to care for them. It is rarely what they planned to be doing at this point in their lives and almost always the result of one or several tragedies.

You Are Not Alone

If you find yourself caring for one or more of your grandchildren, you are probably going through a wide range of emotions. Second-time parents often feel isolated. This is perfectly natural. It is important to remember, however, that you are not alone. There are millions of people in the same situation.

Although many believe that "grandparents as parents" are found only among poor, nonwhite city dwellers, this is far from true. More than half of the children being cared for by their grandparents are white, and many are neither poor nor live in cities. Family tragedies may strike some groups more frequently, but no group is immune.

According to the U.S. Bureau of the Census, there are more than 4 million children under age eighteen living in their grandparents' home today—an increase of more than 1.7 million over 1980! Moreover, more than one-third of these children (1.4 million) are in their grandparents' custody because no (middle-generation) parent is present or capable of caring for them. And these figures probably underestimate the situation. Many grandparents are ashamed to admit that their children are inadequate parents and deny their role as full-time caregivers, claiming it is only a temporary arrangement. The figures also don't count "day-care grandparents," who provide regular daily care but live in a separate house or apartment, or grandparents who live in the parent's house but are responsible for most of the child care. According to some experts, children living with at least one grandparent make up one of every twenty American households. That's 5 percent, an average of one household on every block. If, as some claim, the American family is in crisis, grandparents are being called upon to shoulder a huge part of the burden. (This is not a solely American phenomenon. In many parts of Africa, AIDS is called the "grandmothers' disease" because the burden of caring for the sick and the survivors falls on these older women.)

In this chapter, I am primarily concerned with those grand-parents who either temporarily or permanently assume the functions of a parent. If there is a positive side to the existence of so many second-time parents, it is that there has also been an increase in resources and understanding. At last count, there were more than 400 grandparent support groups in the United States. Many are chapters or offshoots of national organizations, a list of which appears at the end of this book. If there isn't a group near you, they can also assist you in forming a group of your own.

Check Out Your Options

When family tragedy strikes, all your instincts may be shout-ing that you *have* to be the one to care for your grandchildren. Consider your options carefully. Raising your grandchildren should be a conscious choice, not something that just happens. If you are married (75 percent of grandparent caretakers are), it should be a joint decision, not a *fait accompli* imposed by one grandparent on another. Perhaps there is another family member, another son or daughter with children, who can care for this child instead of you or at least share the responsibility.

Parenting your grandchildren means giving up most of what is special and fun about grandparenting: you won't be able to spoil them or send them home when you are tired. You'll have many more conflicts and will be responsible for discipline, medical care, and their education. And whatever the reasons why your adult children can't care for their chil-dren, your grandchildren are probably going to need lots of attention and help. Although researchers are still uncertain about what kinds of difficulties are the products of seeds sown under their parents' care and what kinds result from the disruption of family structure and role confusion, children raised by their grandparents often have learning and behavioral troubles in school.

The first thing that you have to ask yourself is: Can I really take care of my grandchild until she's an adult? Before answering that question, you may need to talk to some experts for advice. Although no one can offer you any guarantees, a good person to start with is your doctor. You won't have the same energy you had as a young parent, but you need to be *reasonably healthy* to care for an active child or adolescent. Not surprisingly, 75 percent of custodial grandparents are under age sixty-four, with more than a third under age fifty-five. Go to your doctor for a checkup and ask about a suitable exercise plan. Although many grandparents have actually started taking better care of themselves—giving up smoking, for example—in order to carry out their custodial roles, many others simply try to ignore their difficulties. It is a good idea to at least begin with an objective medical opinion on your situation.

Your accountant or financial counselor (if you don't have one, now may be the time to find one) can give you some idea if you can afford the financial burden. The unfixed expenses of raising a child can be quite a strain, especially if you are living on a fixed income. As Anne Bancroft cynically comments in the 1996 film *Homecoming*, in which she plays a widowed grandmother taking care of her four orphaned grandchildren, "I had some money put aside for my old age, but after my last trip to the store to buy groceries, I realized that I'm going to have to die a month earlier than I'd planned." Although assistance is available through various government agencies, it usually covers only a fraction of your real expenses.

You should also consider whether your house, apartment, neighborhood, and community have the basic institutions, such as school and medical care, necessary to raise a child. Many retirement communities lack the facilities that children require, and some have even legislated against their presence. A recent issue of *Vital Connections* (*The Grandparenting Newsletter*) quoted an Associated Press story of a sixteen-year-old who went to live with his grandparents in (the ironically named!) Youngstown, Arizona, to escape his abusive stepfather. City age ordinances forbid people age eighteen or under from staying in a household for more than three months. Despite their grandson's obvious need and his demonstrated good conduct, his grandparents were able to get only temporary permission for him to stay.

Expecting the Unexpected

Second-time parents usually find themselves on an emotional roller coaster. Just when you thought that your life had settled down, your dreams are dashed; your work and social life are disrupted, your retirement nest egg eroded.

The pressures of caring for young children also take a heavy toll on grandparents' marriages. Even if you were able to agree to care for your grandchild without too much rancor, the day-to-day stresses of coping with young children can challenge any marriage. Whatever disagreements there may have been in the past regarding the best way to raise your children will probably recur with your grandchildren and may be heightened by new issues. If one of you wants to continue to be the protective grandparent and leaves the other to be the stern parental figure, it's a recipe for resentment. "Good cop, bad cop" may be an effective interrogation technique, but if the grandparent trying to draw the line is always being undermined by the other grandparent, no one benefits.

The 1994 movie *Seasons of the Heart*, starring Carol Burnett and George Segal, provides a particularly moving account of a vibrant couple, both in their early sixties whose recent marriage is thrown into turmoil when her drug-addicted daughter abandons her young son. Although their financial situation and health are such that caring for a child poses no immediate problems of that sort, it disrupts their lives and threatens their relationship. The daughter's brief and abortive attempt to take her son back only serves to confuse him and his grandmother.

If you have decided to care for your grandchild, almost every aspect of your new situation will probably test the stability of your marriage. Many parents find dealing with their adult child to be the most difficult part of the process. When grandparents raise a grandchild, the child's parent may become like an older sibling and may compete for the grandparents' attention. You will have to present a united front in dealing with your adult child on such issues as whether she can move back home, how often she can see her child, and whether you should go to court to have her declared an unfit parent.

Although the term "sandwich generation" was coined to refer to adult children caught between their children and their parents, grandparents caring for their grandchildren are really the ones caught in the middle. Usually they are torn between their desire to protect their grandchild and yet not abandon their own adult child, their grandchild's parent. Often they find that devoting so much time and energy to a grandchild or child takes its toll on their relationships with their other adult children and grandchildren. Many custodial grandparents report not seeing their other grandchildren as often as they would like and feel guilty over this comparative lack of closeness and involvement.

It is not surprising anxiety, depression, and loneliness are common complaints of many custodial grandparents. Though many grandparents express tremendous relief that they no longer have to worry about the daily safety and welfare of their grandchildren, they continue to be troubled by the plight of their adult children. In caring for your grandchild, it is vital that your equip yourself with as broad and reliable a support system as possible.

Guilt: It's not your fault. Modern psychology has certainly contributed a great deal to our understanding of human behavior. However, one of the less positive features of modern psychology is a massive flight from responsibility. Sometimes it seems that any time people are caught acting irresponsibly, they shift the blame to someone or something else. It is not their fault; television, movies, the educational system, and of course their parents are at fault.

Unless your adult child died in an accident or from an illness, one of the questions that is going to hover in the background is "What did I do wrong?" Judges, social workers, friends, and you yourself may all be wondering if this is somehow your fault. Do not buy into this. In the words of Sylvie de Toledo, social worker, author, and founder of Grandparents as Parents, "No one makes a person take drugs, abandon a baby, or abuse a child. Whatever choices you made as parents are past you. You did the best you could. Your children are now adults, and they are making their own choices."

Caring for Your Grandchild: A Few Tips

Caring for your grandchild as if you were a parent is just that and nothing less. It would take a whole book, or even several, to update you on everything you need to know about raising a child today. You will need to update yourself with the latest wisdom on everything from pacifiers to pediatricians. You will have to become more familiar with your local school system than you ever imagined. And those are just the more obvious topics. Your best bet is to contact your support group for some tips and pick up some of the recommended books.

There are also some special issues in raising grandchildren. A proper medical exam is just as important for your grandchild as it is for you. One of the first things you should do is take him to a pediatrician for a complete physical. If at all possible, you should get hold of his medical records. (You usually will need legal custody of your grandchild to take him to a doctor.) I know that sometimes this is not possible. If your grandson has been neglected, he may not have been receiving regular immunizations, so it is important to bring these up-to-date. If he has been a victim of abuse, a medical exam is vital for documenting past injuries or signs of mistreatment. And finally, a proper checkup should reveal any preexisting medical conditions.

Perhaps the most heartbreaking situation of all is when your grandchild has been exposed to drugs while in the womb. Unless your daughter or daughter-in-law was taking drugs almost right until the birth, they may not show up in the newborn. If you suspect this to be the case, however, you should discuss it with a physician as soon as possible. Drug-exposed children often suffer from a variety of medical difficulties as they grow up, from neurological damage to hyperactivity.

Your grandchild's emotional and spiritual well-being is no less important than her physical health. However difficult and painful you may find the crisis with your adult child, it's even harder on your grandchildren. You have a lifetime of experience to fall back upon to help you cope with this new reality; they are much more vulnerable. While you may have learned appropriate ways to express your grief, anger, guilt, and fear, your grandchild may need to express all of these feelings and others that are not quite so easy to interpret. Many children who have been abandoned or abused adopt behaviors generally found in much younger children. These may include bedwetting, baby talk, and clinging. Sleep and eating disorders are also quite common.

Even if things are fairly calm at home, your grandchild may have difficulties in school. Although stability and continuity are vital in these situations, often there is no choice but to move your grandchild into a new school closer to where you live. Being the new kid in school is never easy, especially if you come in after the school year is under way and groups have formed and friendships have been made. If at all possible, you may want to keep your granddaughter in the same school, even if it means a little extra driving for a few months. You can make the changes when things at home are a little more settled or at the start of the next school year. Of course, you often have no choice about such things.

Even if your grandchild stays in the same school, children can be very cruel, and joking about another child's mother or father can take on unintended dimensions when the parents are absent. Schools tend to presume a parent-child child unit, so it is best to let them know as soon as possible about your situation. This will also alert everyone to watch for behavioral problems such as fighting, absences, withdrawn behavior, or a sudden drop in grades. Troublemakers are much easier to spot than quiet kids, who tend to get lost in the shuffle, so keep your eyes and ears open.

Unfortunately, there are no easy solutions to many of these problems. Often they will begin to lessen as your grandchild gets used to a more stable, caring, and nurturing environment. This means providing a household where reassurance and consistency are just a way of life. Hugs, regular mealtimes and bedtimes, and lots and lots of patience and understanding are only the beginning. No one expects you to do this all by yourself, so look to other family members, friends, support groups, and professionals for help and support.

One of the questions that all parenting grandparents have to face is what to tell their grandchildren about their parents. On this issue as in others—including sex education or death (see Chapter 13)—my advice is to make use of "measured" truth. That means you have to find a way to tell the truth in a manner appropriate to your particular grandchild's age and ability to understand. Saying that a parent is addicted to drugs won't mean much to a three-year-old, but it may confirm something that your teenage granddaughter already suspects.

One of the great things about telling the truth is that you don't have to remember what you have said or worry that someone else will inadvertently let the cat out of the bag. Lying to your grandchild about her parents is an invitation for trouble. Children have a way of finding out secrets, and your grandson has probably been disappointed by the adults around him often enough without your risking doing it again. Of course, you need to be tactful and sensitive.

Make It Easy on Yourself

All of the issues discussed in this chapter thus far give only a hint of the challenges you are going to be facing. Anything you can do to make your life easier without sacrificing your grandchildren's safety and well-being is highly recommended. Regular schedules, chore assignments, and clearly set bedtimes will all make your life easier. It may be that when you were raising your children it never would have occurred to you bring in fast food or microwave a frozen dinner, but it can save you a lot of work—and your grandson will probably consider it quite a treat.

All in all, you may find that your new parenting routine is very different from what you experienced with your own children. Your children may have participated in lots of after-school activities and so you spent much of your time carpooling. With your grandchildren, you just may not have the time or the resources. There's no shame in saying so. You may have shunned day care or after-school programs when you were a parent, but now they may be the only way for you to get the free time you need to rest, relax, see friends, and take care of yourself. It's important not to be a prisoner of the past and hold yourself hostage to your previous standards.

Even if your doctor gave you the green light to begin taking care of your grandchildren, it's a good idea to get regular checkups. You should also be sure to find time to rest. One of the best ways to do this is to take your grandchild to an activity, such as a story time at the library or an activity at the local

Y or community center where other adults take charge. At first you may want to hang around, but eventually you may be able to use the time to rest, run errands, or have a quiet cup of coffee with a friend.

If you're married, be sure that you and your spouse still find time alone together. Caring for young children, especially when it is not what you expected to be doing, can take a tremendous toll on your family life. Do not sacrifice your marriage to save your grandchildren.

Thus far, I have been looking at some of the practical and emotional issues that arise when you're a custodial grandparent. As I have tried to stress, this is usually a difficult situation, almost always the result of one or several family tragedies. Unfortunately, this is only a small part of the story. Caring for your grandchildren also involves you in a maze of legal and financial issues that are never easy and often make the experience even more stressful and draining. Given the complexity of these issues, I can really only scratch the surface here. *Be sure you contact legal and financial professionals or get information from some other reliable source, such as the groups listed at the end of this chapter.*

Protective Services

There are few situations that cause more anguish to grandparents than when they suspect that a parent is physically, sexually, or mentally abusing a child. You want to protect your grandchild, but you don't want to get your son or daughter in trouble. In many cases, you may not really be certain of the situation because you have only indirect evidence, such as bruises or other indications. Or perhaps you believe that your son or daughter is using drugs or engaging in other behavior that endangers your grandchild.

The one thing that you can certainly *not* do is ignore the situation. This is the one glaring exception to the rule that grandparents should leave major child-care decisions to the parents! If you suspect abuse, begin to keep a record of incidents. You may need it to prove your case. The best solution is to find a way to intervene with the parents that will lead them to seek help and stop the abuse. If they deny the problem, however, and are not willing to seek counseling or other help, you may have no choice but to contact outside help and report your fears.

In every state, at least part of the child welfare agency is devoted to protecting children from abuse and neglect. Often called Child Protective Services (CPS), it becomes involved when a family asks for help or when someone else, such as a neighbor, school nurse, or grandparent reports that a child is in danger. Working through the (usually juvenile) courts, hearings are held to determine if the allegations are true and, if so, how to protect the child.

Because of the importance the authorities assign to the safety of children, child welfare agencies have extraordinary powers. Once they have been called in, they are in to stay. You can't just ask them to go away or tell them that you don't need their help. If the case worker determines that your grandchild is at risk, she may remove her from her parents' care. Although the agency may ask you to care for the child, this is by no means automatic. Hearings will be held to determine the best interests of the child.

Unless they are the ones filing the report, grandparents usually become involved with CPS after their grandchild is already in the system. While hearings are being held to determine how best to protect the child, the state takes over legal custody while deciding to whom to assign physical custody. Although this sounds fairly simple and straightforward, it's not an accident that many grandparents see CPS as their worst nightmare. As with so many social service agencies, CPS is understaffed and overworked. Your family loses its privacy and finds itself at the mercy of strangers. For example, you may have been caring for your grandchildren informally for months or even years. If you turn to CPS to prevent an abusive parent from taking the child home on weekends or otherwise endangering your grandchild, there is no guarantee that you will be successful. Child welfare laws clearly favor parents over grandparents, and the authorities may attempt to reunite parent and child, sometimes after years of abandonment. Even if the authorities decide that your grandchild does not belong with her parent, they could decide that you are too old, in too poor health, or otherwise not suitable to care for her. Finally, even if your grandchild continues to live with you, your family will be subjected to an unprecedented level of scrutiny through caseworker visits.

Making It Legal

Although your sense of family may make your decision to care for your grandchild seem obvious, in a legal sense it is far more complex. As I discussed in Chapter 11 regarding divorce, grandparents have comparatively few legal rights. One immediate consequence of this is that once you've decided to care for your grandchild, you have little choice but to involve yourself in the legal system. If you have never been involved with the courts, be prepared for an often harrowing experience. In fact, even if you have been to court before, it may not have prepared you adequately for what many custodial grandparents face.

One of the terms you're going to hear over and over again is *custody*. People use this word in a variety of ways, so to avoid a great deal of confusion I would like to start by making a simple distinction: *Physical custody* means that you are the person the child lives with. It is actually more of a description of a situation than a formal legal position. *Legal custody* means that you have the responsibility and authority under the law to make decisions regarding the daily affairs (school, medical care, etc.) of the child.

Physical custody is one of the most common arrangements for grandparents who are caring for their grandchildren. Often it just evolves when grandparents begin looking after their grandchildren for longer and longer periods until one day it becomes the standard arrangement. It requires no intervention of the courts, no lawyers' fees, no social workers. As tempting as it may be to continue to care for your grandchildren on an informal basis (some people call this informal custody), this setup offers neither you nor your grandchild much protection. So long as you have *only* physical custody, you and your granddaughter are subject to her parents' whims and wishes because they retain legal custody. Even if your grandchild's parents have agreed to place her with you, they can remove her legally any time they want. Not only is this not what you want in the case of an addicted or abusive parent, but it perpetuates your grandchild's insecurity if she doesn't know where she will be for a certainty. In addition, if you have only physical custody, you may have trouble registering your grandchild for school or getting her medical care if she requires treatment.

For all these reasons, almost all authorities recommend that you secure some form of legal custody if you are going to be caring for your grandchild. In most states there are three ways of doing this. Each of them has advantages and disadvantages with regard to duration, the amount of control you will have, the degree of court involvement, and the extent to which parental rights are limited or suspended. Although some aspects of gaining custody can be handled without a lawyer, this is the exception rather than the rule. Even if your attempt to obtain legal custody is unopposed, you would be well advised to hire an attorney. We all know the saying that "a person who represents himself has a fool as a lawyer." In this case, the goal is to protect your grandchild, and you don't want her to have a fool representing her!

Custody Orders

A custody order will give you the right to see to most of your grandchild's daily needs, such as health care and school enrollment, without having to challenge the parent's fitness or basic rights as a parent. You can, however, ask to limit the number or type (supervised or unsupervised) of visits.

This is usually a good approach if you feel that one of the parents can still play a useful, supportive role in your grandchild's life or if you have a genuine reason to believe that the situation is temporary. Once you have a custody order, your grandchild's parent will have to go to court to get it changed if she wants to regain custody. This usually means that she will have to show that this is in the best interest of the child and that her situation has changed. The exact process varies from state to state.

Guardianship

When you apply for guardianship, you are asking the courts to *temporarily* suspend parental rights so that you can care for your grandchild. As the child's legal guardian, you have both physical and legal custody. Not only can you handle arrangements such as medical care and school enrollment, but subject to court ordered visitation rights, you also determine if and when your grandchild sees his parents.

Although, in many cases, guardianship is not all that different from a custody order, it can be a much more complicated and costly process. Under guardianship, you have physical and legal custody of your grandchild because his parents are considered unfit. In order to suspend parental rights in this manner, you will have to prove that the parents are unwilling to or incapable of caring for their child. In effect, you are building and then presenting a case against your adult children in order to protect your grandchild. If you win, your child has been legally declared unfit; if you lose, your relationship with your child may have been ruined for nothing.

A guardianship order can often be costly, especially if the parents or some other relative (such as the other grandparents) contest it in court. Also, there are some benefits that you can receive only if your grandchild remains dependent upon the court. Finally, even if you manage to obtain guardianship, it is never permanent until the child reaches age eighteen. The parents or other relatives can always appeal to the courts if they can prove that this is in the best interests of the child.

Adoption

In some circumstances, adoption may be the best form of legal custody for you and your grandchild. If you adopt your grandchild, you will have all the legal rights and responsibilities of a birthparent. In fact, adoption, unlike guardianship, *permanently* dissolves all legal ties between your grandchild and her parents and creates a new child-parent unit. You are, in effect, no longer her grandparents but her parents. This does not mean that your grandchild will never see her birthparents again, but it does mean that you have the right to decide if, when, and under what circumstances. For this reason, adoption is the most secure form of custody possible.

If all of the above makes it sound as if I am recommending adoption for all or even most couples, let me make it clear that this is definitely not the case. As with all the options discussed previously, you need to ask yourself if this is the best solution for your grandchild. The questions I raised before regarding your emotional, financial, and physical ability to raise a child until adulthood become all the more vital in this case.

For adoption as for guardianship, unless your grandchild has been orphaned or her parents readily consent, you will have to go to court to prove that your child is unfit to be a parent. Unlike guardianship, you will be asking for a permanent ruling, not merely a temporary decision. Many people find it hard to give up on their adult child, even when they know it is in the best interest of their grandchild.

The adoption process can also be very expensive. If the parent opposes your effort, there are trial costs. Unless your grandchild is eligible for a special-needs adoption subsidy, even an uncontested adoption can be expensive. One woman I know had been caring for her grandchild for several years but still had to pay lawyer's fees, court costs, and even for home visits to evaluate her fitness as a parent. You must also remember that adoption will end the birthparents' obligation of child support.

Paying the Bills

No matter how much you love your grandchildren and how obligated you feel toward them, you are not responsible for supporting them financially. Financial support is the parents' responsibility. If they cannot or will not meet their obligations, their children are entitled to government assistance. Before you insist that you don't want charity or welfare, remember that your grandchildren are entitled to this money. Do not let your pride or your ignorance of their rights deny them the help to which they are entitled.

Receiving government aid means working your way through the red tape, arbitrariness, and lack of clear information that characterize many bureaucracies. At times you may feel like throwing your hands up in disgust and just walking away. Don't. If your grandchildren qualify for assistance, they deserve it, and you should make every effort to see that they receive it.

In the pages that follow I am going to give only a capsule description of the different assistance programs for which you and your grandchildren may qualify. *Grandparents as Parents: A Survival Guide for Raising a Second Family*, an excellent guide by Sylvie de Toledo and Deborah Elder Brown, offers more detailed information. Always keep in mind that programs are usually administered by the state, county, and city and will differ from locality to locality. In addition, many of the programs are subject to change every time welfare or health reform laws are implemented.

Consult your local authorities and especially local grandparent support groups for up-to-date information. The support groups should be particularly helpful in determining the hidden costs of the various programs. Foster care benefits are comparatively high but usually result in much more court involvement in your family life. Obtaining guardianship or adopting your grandchildren gives you far more control over their lives but usually results in the loss of government benefits.

Aid to Families with Dependent Children (AFDC)

AFDC is the major child welfare program in the United States. It provides monthly payments by check to help children in need. Most of the recipients are minor children living in single-parent (usually female-headed) households. In 1994 there were approximately 14 million people on AFDC, of whom two-thirds were children. Although parent caretakers must qualify for AFDC under conditions set out by the federal and state governments, these income limits do not apply to other relative caretakers, including grandparents. Since most officials dealing with AFDC are accustomed to dealing with parents who must prove financial eligibility, it is important that you remind them that as a grandparent, *you don't have to be low-income for your children to qualify for AFDC.*

If, however, you are low-income, you may wish to be included in the AFDC benefits. In this case, your income and financial situation will be considered. If you qualify to receive AFDC *with* your grandchildren, it will mean that you will get Medicaid coverage as well. In some states, it may also mean a slightly larger monthly payment.

Since only relative caretakers can obtain AFDC benefits, you will have to prove that you are the children's grandparent. Although this may seem a minor point and rather obvious to you, remember to bring written documentation.

Obtaining AFDC benefits for your grandchildren can be yet another source of tension between you and their parents. For example, if they have been receiving these benefits, that will stop when you prove that the child lives with you. In some cases, parents try to take their children back in order to retain control over the benefits. If they *have* continued to receive these payments after their child is no longer living with them, this is fraud, and they are (at least in theory) liable for prosecution.

When you apply for AFDC benefits, you will be required to certify that your grandchildren have been denied parental support. From the government's perspective, taxpayers' money is being used to fulfill the parents' obligations. The parents continue to be liable, and authorities may attempt to force them to pay child support. You will usually have to give the authorities information to help them locate the parents. In most cases, government efforts to force parents, especially "deadbeat dads," to pay child support have been minimal, but some states have begun to strengthen their efforts in this direction. In most cases, if the state is successful in collecting, it will share a portion of the money with you. Of course, if your grandchild's father is *forced* to provide some support, whether immediately or in later years, this can become another source of tension between parents and grandparents.

Foster Care Benefits

Foster care benefits are a type of AFDC for children who have been removed from their homes by protective services and are living somewhere else. Up until 1979, children cared for by relatives (including grandparents) were denied these benefits. However, in a landmark case, *Miller* v. *Youakim*, the Supreme Court ruled that this was improper. Because of this case, these benefits are often referred to as *Youakim*, but some states refer to them as federal, relative, or family foster care. Although this decision has been on the books for almost twenty years, many social workers still neglect to inform relatives of these benefits.

Children are often eligible for either AFDC or *Youakim*, and the latter often provides higher benefits. However, your grandchild will be eligible for these benefits only if she has been placed with you by the court. Since the courts are often slow to act, many grandparents choose to protect their grandchildren and receive lesser benefits rather than put them at the mercy of the court's discretion. Fortunately, the decision to apply for benefits is not irreversible. You can apply for and receive regular AFDC and later apply for *Youakim*. (The increased benefits are not retroactive, however.)

Your grandchild is eligible for *Youakim* only so long as he is a dependent of the court. This means that if you become his legal guardian, you are usually no longer eligible for this program, although he may still qualify for AFDC. In short, you may have to choose between greater control and greater benefits.

Medicaid

The Medicaid program assists with health care costs for persons with low incomes and limited assets. Most grandchildren being raised by grandparents qualify, and in many states Medicaid comes automatically with AFDC and Social Security Insurance (SSI). If your grandchildren do not qualify for AFDC but have lots of medical bills, they may also qualify if your state has special rules that allow them to qualify as medically needy.

Social Security Survivor's Benefits

If you're like most people, Social Security means retirement benefits. But Social Security also pays survivor's benefits to minor children. In fact, 98 percent of minor children qualify for survivor's benefits if a working parent dies. If your grandchild's parent worked, paid Social Security taxes, and earned enough credits to qualify, his or her children are probably eligible for a monthly insurance payment. The precise benefits will vary according to the parent's work history. Since benefits are usually retroactive to the date on which you applied, it is a good idea to call your local Social Security office as soon as possible.

Food Stamps

The Food Stamp program helps low-income households to buy food. While many households who receive AFDC also receive food stamps, the eligibility rules are very different. In determining whether your grandchildren qualify for food stamps and, if so, how much, officials will consider the income of everyone who lives in your household.

It Ain't Over Till It's Over!

Unless you have adopted your grandchild or both parents are dead, you can never be sure that he will stay with you permanently. The less formal your custody arrangement, the easier it will be for the parents to reclaim their child. If you have legal custody, especially guardianship, it will be somewhat harder for the parents to get their child back because the burden of proof will be on them to prove that they are capable of caring for their child. Still, the court system favors the parents, and you have no guarantees. Moreover, once a parent regains custody, you can no longer be sure of even visitation rights!

Under a worst-case scenario, the parent can seek to exclude you totally from your grandchild's life. As discussed previously, many of the steps you will have taken to protect and support your grandchild, such as seeking guardianship or AFDC payments, may have strained your relationship with his father or mother. This is especially common if you've gone to court to have the parent declared unfit, but it can happen even when the court, rather than the grandparent, has taken the initiative. If your adult child has resettled in another state, your grandchild may be moved there, which will seriously curtail your contact.

If your child has really taken charge of his life and licked the problems that led him to abandon his child or have him taken away, your feelings will be mixed: relief that your adult child has once again become a functioning responsible parent, sadness that you are losing a child who has become so much a part of your life, and concern and fear that your child may not be able to maintain a safe and nurturing home environment.

Your grandchild may also be plagued by uncertainty. Although there will often be a certain happiness at returning to his mother, his memories of past disappointments, mistreatment, and injuries will not disappear. Some children strongly oppose being sent back to their parents, and you may find yourself the target of the anger through no fault of your own. At the least, your lame duck status, may lead to behavioral problems reminiscent of the first days of your parenting.

If you have advance warning of the hand-over, you can take the time to prepare both yourself and your grandchild. Although you would certainly hope that all will be well, you need to be sure that your grandchild knows how to contact the authorities in the event that his parent returns to dangerous behavior. If the parents have allowed you to stay in contact with your grandchild, be sure he knows how to contact you in the case of an emergency.

Once you have prepared yourself and your grandchild for the transition, there is very little you can do of immediate impact. If you are still able to see your grandchild, you will be able to watch the situation and, if your relationship with your adult child is good, help provide continuity. Unfortunately, you also need to keep an eye open for signs of dangerous or irresponsible behavior.

Even if you found caring for your grandchild physically, emotionally, and financially taxing, you will almost certainly feel a letdown when she leaves. It is perfectly normal to grieve, and you should turn to your friends and other family members for support. After a period of mourning, you will need to get on with your life. This may be your opportunity to return to the social activities you had to give up when you were caring for a young child or teenager. Some grandparents have found solace in their community's foster grandparent programs, which allow them to mentor local children. Others, motivated by their experience with child welfare, the court system, and AFDC, have become political activists, organizing other grandparents and lobbying for grandparents' rights.

Remember, it ain't over till it is over. Children may be returned to their parents only to become ping-pong balls, traveling back and forth at the whim of the parents and the courts. However much you may miss them, the last thing you want to have happen is for your grandchildren to be returned to you by the child welfare agency. It means your adult child has failed yet again as a parent and your grandchild has suffered yet further mistreatment and harm.

Little Moments of Joy and Love

Throughout most of this chapter I have discussed the daily difficulties and challenges you face when you take on the role of custodial grandparent. Given the tragic circumstances that lead most grandparents to care for their grandchildren, it is hardly surprising that, almost without exception, they would prefer that their situation was different.

But this doesn't mean that it is all bad news. There is a Jewish tradition that a person who saves a single soul is considered to have saved an entire world. Many grandparents feel tremendous satisfaction that they have been able to provide a safe and secure home for their grandchildren. Although they are often tired, they report feeling rejuvenated and finding a new purpose in life in their golden years.

Although it isn't the life you would have chosen for either you or your grandchildren, at the end of a long day when you are worn out and they have been tucked in, the simple words "I love you, Grandma" can make it all seem worth the sacrifice.

Further Reading and Resources

DE TOLEDO, SYLVIE, and DEBORAH EDLER BROWN. *Grandparents as Parents: A Survival Guide for Raising a Second Family* (New York and London: The Guilford Press, 1995).

DOUCETTE-DUDMAN, DEBORAH, and JEFFREY R. LACURE. *Raising Our Children's Children* (Fairview Press, 1996).

Grandparents as Parents (GAP)
P.O. Box 964
Lakewood, CA 90174
310-924-3996
310-839-2548
Fax: 714-828-1375

Grandparents Raising Grandchildren
P.O. Box 104
Colleyville, TX 76034
817-577-0435

Grandparents United for Children's Rights
137 Larkin St.
Madison, WI 53705
608-238-8751

Grandsrus
Grandparents and Special Others Raising Children
www.grandrus.com
This Web site provides support and comfort for grandparents and "special others" between ages 40 and 80 who are caring for children. It is not a legal service but provides connections to other Web sites for legal advice.

MINKLER, MEREDITH, and KATHLEEN M. ROE. *Grandmothers as Caregivers: Raising the Children of the Crack Cocaine Epidemic* (Family Caregiver Applications Series, vol. 2) (Beverly Hills, CA: Sage, 1993).

National Foster Parent Association
9 Dartmoor Drive
Crystal Lake, IL 60014
815-455-2527

The National Grandparent Information Center
AARP Headquarters
601 E St. NW
Washington, DC 20049
202-434-2296, 9:00 a.m. to 5:00 p.m. EST weekdays
www.aarp.org

ROCKING/Raising Our Children's Kids:
An Intergenerational Network of Grandparenting, Inc.
P.O. Box 96
Niles, MI 49120
616-683-9038

Second Time Around Parents
Family and Community Services of Delaware County
100 W. Front St.
Media, PA 19063

TAKAS, MARIANNE. *Grandparents Raising Grandchildren: A Guide to Finding Help and Hope.* (New York: Brookdale Foundation Group, 1995).
This booklet provides sources to turn to for help and support. It is available for $3.00 to cover postage and handling from:

Relatives as Parents Program (RAPP)
The Brookdale Foundation Group
126 East 56th St.
New York, NY 10011-3668

13

Like a Passing Shadow

O Lord, What is man, that You should care about him,
mortal man, that You should think of him?
Man is like a breath;
his days are like a passing shadow.

Psalm 144: 3-4

As I said at the outset, this is not a book about aging. Although the subject has been touched upon here and there, it has not been a major focus of the book. Yet it would be impossible for me to complete the task I have set myself without saying a few words about aging and death and your relationship with your grandchildren.

A University of Southern California anthropologist, Barbara Myerhoff, was perhaps the first person to properly document the special culture of the elderly in America. As she documented so movingly in her book *Number Our Days*, the elderly Jews from Venice, California, she studied had many lessons to teach her and, in a wider sense, all of us. So many passages from this book (it was also the basis for an Academy Award–winning documentary) moved me that it is difficult to choose only one to share. But the following captures much of what I wish to say about aging and the younger generations:

> I see old people now in a new way, as part of me, not 'they'. Most normal, relatively sensitive people identify naturally with children. They remember what it was like to have been a child themselves and as a result *see* children—are aware of them as a part of life, appreciative of their specific needs, rights, and characteristics. But in our culture today, we do not have this same natural attentiveness to and empathy with the elderly, in part because they are not among us, and no doubt they are not among us because we don't want to recognize the inevitability of our own future decline and dependence. An insidious circularity has developed—ignorance, based in part on denial of our future, leading to fear and rejection of the elderly, engendering guilt that is often expressed as neglect or mistreatment, then more guilt, avoidance, and ignorance; ageism is characterized by the same self-fulfilling processes that operate in racism. . . .
>
> What the Center people taught me went beyond knowledge about old age. In addition they provided a model of an alternative life-style, built on values in many ways antithetical to those commonly esteemed by contemporary Americans. . . . It was built on their veneration for their religious and cultural membership and it was full of meaning, intensity, and consciousness. . . . It was especially their passion for meaning that appealed to me so deeply.

By immersing herself in the lives of the elderly, Myerhoff took to wearing heavy gloves and shoes, removing her glasses, or blocking her ears to develop an appreciation for their daily physical reality. She was able to stop seeing them as the "other" and recognize them as part of herself. (Her statement—"I would be a little old Jewish lady one day"—is tinged with irony and sadness, since she died an untimely death at a young age.)

Chances are that your grandchildren will have very few opportunities to really become acquainted with other people your age as individuals. It is especially important, therefore, that you provide them with an exemplar—a shining example of all that older people can be. Despite the efforts of various organizations, ageism is still one of the most pernicious forms of discrimination in our society today. Stereotypes about aging and the elderly are still purveyed on a daily basis in print, on television, and in the movies. Hardly a day goes by without Jay Leno, David Letterman, and their less successful imitators trying to get laughs at the expense of senior citizens. The sexuality of the elderly is made fun of, their physical difficulties are the subject of caricature, and their memories are the topic of cruel humor.

Under such circumstances, one of the most valuable gifts we can give our grandchildren is a model of the elderly that contradicts these uninformed stereotypes. We can serve as a reminder that older people can be experienced, intelligent, and inquisitive. In most cases, this model will stay with your grandchildren long after you are gone and influence their interactions with their elders for the rest of their lives.

In the future, when people look back on the twentieth century, I think our attitudes toward the aged will be one of the things that will most puzzle and appall them. In particular, they will find it hard to understand how, in an age of so much technological progress designed to minimize the need for physical effort (the automobile, telephone, computer, etc.), we could still continue almost automatically to connect physical strength with mental ability. They will wonder how, in the century that produced the renowned physicist Stephen Hawkings, we could continue to automatically discount older people with much lesser physical challenges than his as "past their prime".

One of the lessons that all of us need to learn for ourselves and teach our grandchildren is that the diminishment of our physical prowess does not mean a lessening of our ability to advise, support, cherish, and love. Significantly, none of the roles I discussed in Chapter 5 are dependent on your physical strength.

This is not to minimize the real toll that age and illness can take on our lives. It is, rather, a call not to let them rob us of our right to grandparent. Although there may be some pressure from your grandchild's parents to "spare him" and cut back on your visits if you are not well, it is important to correct them firmly and gently. Grandparenting can be done from a walker, a rocker, and a bed. If you have concerns about your ability to keep up with your five-year-old grandson, you might consider hiring a local teen to help out by baby-sitting and keeping an eye on things when you need a breather. If you seem to be seeing your granddaughter less because you find the traveling so tiring, suggest that she come to see *you* more often so you'll be better rested. If one grandparent has fewer limitations than another, try to plan your visits so that you both get to spend time with your grandchildren doing different activities.

Facing illness and other adversities with dignity and courage is as valuable as any other lesson you will ever teach your grandchildren. If you can no longer play basketball with your granddaughter or go hiking with your grandson, let them know that you accept your limitations with humor rather than bitterness.

A Death in the Family

Had my circumstances been a little different, this section of this book might never have been written. Most authors who deal with grandparenting have very little to say about death and dying. It is just not a pleasant subject. The primary responsibility for talking to children about the death of a loved one belongs to their parents. And yet the death of a grandparent is likely to be your grandchild's first experience with the mortality of someone she is close to (beloved pets notwithstanding). When your spouse dies, your grandchildren rather naturally may expect you to answer their questions and provide them with guidance as to how to behave. This was driven home to me with a painful immediacy when my husband Fred died last year.

Until comparatively recently, death was (if you'll pardon the expression) a normal part of life. High infant mortality rates and short life expectancies meant that a century ago, children had a much greater familiarity with death than today. The death of siblings was common, and many children lost a parent before they reached adulthood. Only recently has it become likely that someone might reach not only adulthood but even middle age without experiencing the death of a member of their immediate family.

Ironically, while children's *direct* experience of death has declined, their *indirect* experience has increased dramatically. According to recent studies, the average child witnesses thousands of deaths on television by the time he reaches adulthood, and video games include not only graphic violence but often the possibility of accumulating and losing "lives." These deaths are hardly reflective of reality, however. They tend to be quick and violent. Pain, tears, and genuine grief are rarely depicted. Family reactions after the death of a loved one are even rarer.

One current fad, electronic pets, some known as Tamaguchis, die if they are not properly cared for. But far from teaching children about the reality of death, this conveys the strange lesson that death is a temporary condition, easily remedied with the touch of a button. It is not surprising, therefore, that children's electronic experiences of death hardly prepare them for the experience in real life.

Whether upon the death of another family member or in the course of their own illnesses, grandparents can often provide families with a positive model of how to cope with and approach death with dignity and thoughtfulness. The particular messages that you give your grandchildren will depend on your own beliefs and traditions. It's good to discuss the eventuality with your children before it becomes a reality and everyone's emotions are already strained. Many families hesitate to expose their children to a sick or dying grandparent, but most experts agree that children from age five and up can usually deal with the emotions involved in saying goodbye to a grandparent. If your children tell you that they want to protect your grandchildren by keeping them away from you, it is good to be prepared with a knowledge of this fact, backed up by the numerous books on the subject.

Talking to children about death has in many ways been treated in much the same confused way that often characterizes sex education. And I am not just saying that because I have had so much experience talking about sex. In both cases, teachers who have sought to raise the subject with their students have encountered opposition from parents and other authorities, who feel that this is not an appropriate subject for the young. The discussion of death, like sex, in our culture is surrounded by embarrassment, euphemisms, and religious strictures.

In fact, as with sex, children usually let you know when they are curious about the subject. But in the case of a death, you may not have the luxury of waiting for the best time and circumstances. When talking to your grandchild about the death of a loved one, you should be as honest as possible, adapt your message to the age of the particular child, and avoid euphemisms. Reassure her that she is loved and will be cared for no matter how upset her parents or other adults may be. Prepare her for her grief and other feelings and the rituals that are about to take place.

If it is your spouse, son, or daughter who has died, you may not be ready to take on the emotional burden of immediately caring for your grandchild. No one will blame you if you ask another adult to take on this responsibility.

Fortunately, there are several excellent books available on talking to children and helping them cope with death. Although many of these are more concerned with the death of a parent, the information they contain is applicable to other circumstances.

Some fictional accounts that deal specifically with the death of a grandparent are:

Bluenose, P., and W. S. Carpenter. *Two Knots on a Counting Rope* (New York: Holt, 1964), ages 6–9.

Corely, E.A. *Tell Me about Death. Tell Me about Funerals* (Santa Clara, CA: Grammatical Sciences, 1973), ages 8–12.

De Paola, T. *Nana Upstairs and Nana Downstairs* (New York: Putnam, 1973), preschool to age 7.

Mazer, N. *A Figure of Speech* (New York: Delacorte, 1973), age 8 and over.

Miles, M. *Annie and the Old One* (Boston: Little, Brown, 1971), ages 8–12.

Stevens, M. *When Grandpa Died* (Chicago: Children's Press, 1979), preschool to age 7.

Tolan, S.S. *Grandpa—and Me* (New York: Scribner's, 1978), age 8 and over.

Zolotow, C. *My Grandson Lew* (New York: Harper, 1974), ages 4–8.

The keys to talking to your grandchild about death are honesty, understanding, and patience. Ari was the only one of my grandchildren old enough to really understand what was happening when Fred died. He asked his mother, my daughter Miriam, most of his questions. He was also somewhat prepared because a year earlier Fred had suffered a bad stroke, and this time, when it happened again, everybody was upset. His grandfather did not regain consciousness for ten days before he died. I believe that gave us all time to be prepared for the news of his death.

On a lighter note, Ari asked his mother right away if I would get married again. My answer was "not right now"!

One of the most immediate decisions that needs to be made is whether the child should attend the funeral and participate in other mourning rituals. Although many parents and grandparents prefer to exclude children from the mourning, more often than not this is as much to protect themselves as it is a realistic evaluation of the child's needs. When a child is excluded from the funeral, she is denied the right to mourn and share her grief. She may feel that she is being abandoned precisely at the moment when someone she loved has left her. While you may be seeking to protect her, children themselves often resent having been denied the chance to say farewell.

Of course, your grandchild should be given a choice. A child should never be forced to attend a funeral or other memorial service. You or another adult she is close to should explain honestly and clearly what the service and burial will entail. Tell her the meaning and purpose of the ceremonies and what, if any, role may be expected of her. Reassure her that it is natural to be sad, scared, or have all sorts of other strange feelings. Then let her decide. Remember that everyone needs to mourn in his own way and at his own pace.

I *want* my grandchildren to talk about Fred. Leora is too young, and it's sad that neither she nor Michal are going to know him, but they will know about him. Ari is eight and is a very sensitive little boy. Whenever he says something about Fred, I respond immediately.

Final Gifts

While all gifts convey a message, nowhere is this truer than in the case of final legacies. How and when you divide up your possessions is the ultimate statement about your values and concerns.

Whatever your wishes, it is crucial that you arrange your estate in advance. If you don't do this, the courts will. Good estate planning will also ensure that your heirs get as much of your estate as possible and that as little as possible goes to the IRS.

It is also best not to leave your family in the dark about your intentions. This will not ensure that everyone will be happy, but it will give you the opportunity to explain your intentions. This is especially important for personal possessions, such as jewelry, pictures, or other family heirlooms, whose emotional impact may considerably exceed their direct monetary value.

Although no one seems to believe it can happen in their family, everyone knows at least one family that has been torn apart by battles or resentment about inheritance. There are no magic formulas for preventing such disagreements, but the more you plan ahead, the surer you can be that your wishes are clearly understood and carried out.

Although my own personal preference is for charity that begins at home, seeing to your family's needs, but a final bequest to your own favorite cause—a school, public action group, church, or synagogue—is also a fitting statement about your life and your wishes. With these bequests as with others, let your family know of your intentions in advance. It gives you the chance to explain your choices and may avoid confusion at a later date.

Further Reading

BELIN, DAVID W. *Leaving Money Wisely: Creative Estate Planning for Middle- and Upper-Income Americans for the 1990s* (New York: Charles Scribner's Sons, 1990), especially Chapter 4, "Problems of Equity among Grandchildren."

CONDON, GERALD M. and JEFFREY L. *Beyond the Grave: The Right and Wrong Way of Leaving Money to Your Children (and Others)* (New York: Harper Business, 1995).

Afterword

A little more than a decade ago, I published my auto-biography, *All in a Lifetime*. Only in the very last pages did I turn to unfinished business and compile a short "wish list." This is what I wrote: "I would like Joel's being married before too long and I would like to have grandchildren. I would like to write at least one scholarly book. I am still only an associate professor at NYU, and I know that to be a full professor I have to publish an academic book."

Maybe I should have wished for more! I have since published several academic books, and I got that full professorship. Joel is happily married. And I have not one, but three lovely grandchildren!

Of course, not everything has worked out exactly the way I had hoped—Fred's death last year being the most notable case in point. But we had more than thirty-six years together, and I am grateful for that.

In June 1998 I celebrated my seventieth birthday. Six months after that, it will have been sixty years since I last saw my parents and grandmother. As the years rush by, my awareness of how much I carry with me from those first years spent in Frankfurt and Wiesenfeld has only grown. Not only do I continue to see in myself many of the qualities of my parents and grandparents, but I also understand more and more the emotional base they bequeathed to me.

During the sixty years since I last saw my family, I have always managed to see the difficulties I have confronted as challenges and to face life with an intense *joie de vivre*. I know that much of what I experienced since age ten could have left me feeling that the world was a dangerous and uncertain place in which caution was the best policy, yet somehow I have always lived with a tremendous optimism. I believe that to a large extent, this is because of the tremendous happiness I enjoyed and the love I experienced during those crucial early years I shared with my parents and grandparents.

Although many aspects of the world we live in today would doubtless amaze and mystify my parents and grandparents—computers, e-mail, faxes, even television—the importance of the basic values they taught me through both word and deed has not changed. Perhaps without even knowing it, they provided me with the best foundation possible for facing the challenges I was to meet over the next three-score years. Among the most important lessons from them that I continue to carry with me are the power of unconditional love and the importance of family loyalty. I hope I have been able to share this with my children and, more recently, my grandchildren.

Given my busy schedule and how much I love to work and travel, being a good grandmother is not something I can just take for granted. But ever since I went from being just Ruth Westheimer to being "Dr. Ruth," I've always made sure that *I lead my life and don't let my life lead me!* By this I mean that no matter how busy my schedule gets, I make sure that I have the time for the things, and expecially the people, who really matter to me. Another of the lessons that I absorbed at an early age was that there is no time like the present. Perhaps that's one of the reasons why I seem to have so much energy and hate so much to waste time. While still a young child, I learned that the future holds no guarantees and that every moment needs to be cherished and enjoyed to the fullest. This is especially true of your time with those who you love. I lost so much as a child that since then I have made a point of holding on to people—delighting with them when we are together and making sure to keep in touch when we are not.

I am not the kind of person who walks around with a lot of regrets and "should haves." It is just not in my nature. But even if it was, I have tried to build my relationships with each of my grandchildren so that there couldn't possibly be anything to regret. (Maybe this is connected to my own childhood.) I never miss an opportunity to spend time with them. I relish every chance I get to play with them and cherish every extra hug I can get. It seems to me that the time with them just goes by much too fast. They pass from stage to stage and from milestone to milestone in the wink of an eye.

Grandparenting is one of the last adventures I am going to experience, and I do not plan to miss a moment of it. *Neither should you!*

Resources

Associations and Clubs

Foster Grandparents Program
To find a branch near you:
202-606-5000, ext. 199

The Foundation for Grandparenting
Arthur Kornhaber, M.D.
Box 326
Cohasset, MA 02025
gpfound@trail.com
http://www.grandparenting.org

Generations United: A National Coalition on Intergenerational Issues and Programs
c/o CWLA
440 First Street NW
Suite 310
Washington, DC 20001-2085
202-638-2952

Grandparent Classes
Shirley and Robert Strom
College of Education
Arizona State University
Tempe, AZ 85287-0611

Grandparents and Grandchildren's Camp
Sagamore
P.O. Box 146
Raquette Lake, NY 13436
315-354-5311

The Joy of Grandparenting
Clarice A. Orr
7100 Old Post Rd., #20
Lincoln, NE 68506

Today's Young Grandparents Club
Director: Sunie Levin
P.O. Box 11143
Shawnee Mission, KS 66207
1-800-243-5201
Sunielevin@aol.com
This club provides a bimonthly 12-page national newsletter for grandparents, *Your Grandchild*, which provides news and resource information on grandparenting. From planning family reunions to keeping the children busy when they visit or helping out when parents divorce, you'll find ideas that work. For a sample copy of the newsletter, write to the address above.

www.seniornews.com
Includes information on finance, health and wellness, lifestyles, travel, and articles excerpted from *Grand Times Magazine*.

www.seniors-site.com
Articles on grandparenting. Includes guides to books, newsletters, stories by grandkids, stories for grandkids, and information on raising grandchildren.

www.thirdage.com
Family Planet Grandparent's
Gateway
A Web site that is part celebration
of the importance of grandparents,
part advice on the sometimes
thorny byways of family politics.
It includes a photo album of happy
grandfolks and precious babies, a
question and answer column, as
well as parents' and grandparents'
discussion groups.

world.std.com
*Grandloving: Grandparenting with
Activities and Long-Distance Fun*
This Web magazine by Sue Johnson
and Julie Carlson includes tips and
book reviews. See also their book,
*Grandloving: Making Memories with
Your Grandchildren* (Fairview Press),
which contains tips on long-distance
grandparenting, visits, holidays,
family traditions, and over 200 inexpensive and innovative activities.

Bibliography

ADAMAC, CHRISTINE, and W. PIERCE. *The Encyclopedia of Adoption* (New York: Facts of File, 1991).

ADAMS, JANE. *I'm Still Your Mother: How to Get Along with Your Grown-up Children for the Rest of your Life* (New York: Delta Books, 1994).

BELIN, DAVID W. *Leaving Money Wisely: Creative Estate Planning for Middle- and Upper-Income Americans for the 1990s* (New York: Charles Scribner's Sons, 1990), especially Chapter 4, "Problems of Equity among Grandchildren."

BENGSTON, VERN L., and JOAN F. ROBERTSON, Eds. *Grandparenthood* (Beverly Hills, CA: Sage Publications, 1985).

BENNETT, PAULA and WILLIAM H. MEREDITH. "The Modern Role of the Grandmother in China." *International Journal of Sociology of the Family* 25,1 (1995), 1–12.

BILOFSKY, PENNY, and FREDDA SACHAROW. *In-Laws/Outlaws: How to Make Peace with His Family and Yours* (New York: Copestone Press, 1991).

BRODZINSKY, DAVID M., and MARSHALL D. SCHECHTER, Eds. *The Psychology of Adoption* (New York: Oxford University Press, 1990).

CARSON, LILLIAN. *The Essential Grandparent: A Guide to Making a Difference* (Deerfield Beach, FL: Health Communications, 1996).

CARTIER, MICHEL. "Nuclear Versus Quasi-Stem Families: The New Chinese Family Model." *The Journal of Family History* 20,3 (1995): 307–327.

CHERLIN, ANDREW J., and FRANK F. FURSTENBERG, JR. *The New American Grandparent: A Place in the Family, A Life Apart* (New York: Basic Books, 1975).

COHEN, LAWRENCE. "Old Age: Cultural and Critical Perspectives." *Annual Review of Anthropology* 23 (1994): 137–158.

COLE, MICHAEL and SHEILA R. *The Development of Children*, 3rd ed. (New York: W.H. Freeman and Company, 1996).

COONTZ, STEPHANIE. *The Way We Never Were: American Families and the Nostalgia Trap* (New York: Basic Books, 1992).

DUNCAN, GREG J., and KEN R. SMITH. "The Rising Affluence of the Elderly: How Far, How Fair, and How Frail?" *Annual Review of Sociology* 15 (1989): 261–289.

HADDAD, YVONNE YAZBECK, and ADAIR T. LUMMIS. *Islamic Values in the United States* (New York: Oxford University Press, 1987).

HAREVEN, TAMARA K. "Aging and Generational Relations: A Historical and Life Course Perspective." *Annual Review of Sociology* 20 (1994): 437–461.

HESTON, CHARLES. *To Be a Man: Letters to My Grandson* (New York: Simon & Schuster, 1997).

KEITZ, GERALD. *How to Pay for Your Children's College Education.* (Princeton, NJ: The College Board), especially Chapter 4.

KITZINGER, SHEILA. *Becoming a Grandmother: A Life Transition* (New York: Simon & Schuster, 1996).

KORNHABER, ARTHUR, and KENNETH L. WOODWARD. *Grandparents-Grandchildren: The Vital Connection* (New York: Doubleday, 1981).

KORNHABER, ARTHUR, with SONDRA FORSYTH. *Grandpower Power!* (New York: Crown Trade Paperbacks, 1994).

MCDANIEL, ANTONIO. "Historical Racial Differences in Living Arrangements of Children." *Journal of Family History* 19,1 (1994): 57–77.

MERRILL, DEBORAH, and ANN DILL. "Ethnic Differences in Older Mother-Daughter Co-residence." *Ethnic Groups* 8 (1990): 201–213.

MIN, PYONG GAP, Ed. *Asian Americans: Contemporary Trends and Issues* (Thousand Oaks, CA: Sage Publications, 1995).

MOYNIHAN, DANIEL P. *The Negro Family: The Case for National Action* (Washington DC: U.S. Department of Labor, 1965).

MYERHOFF, BARBARA. *Number Our Days* (New York: Simon & Schuster, 1980).

PLATH, DAVID W. *Long Engagements: Maturity in Modern Japan* (Stanford, CA: Stanford University Press, 1980).

RUGGLES, STEVEN. "The Transformation of the American Family Structure." *American Historical Review*, February 1994: 103–128.

SHIMKIN, DEMITRI B., EDITH M. SHIMKIN and DENNIS A. FRATE, Eds. *The Extended Family in Black Societies* (The Hague: Mouton, 1978).

STAHL, ABRAHAM. "The Offspring of Interethnic Marriage: Relations of Children with Paternal and Maternal Grandparents." *Ethnic and Racial Studies* 15,2 (1992): 266–283.

STROM, ROBERT, PAT COLLINGSWORTH, SHIRLEY STROM, DIANNE GRISWOLD, and PARIS STROM. "Evaluating the Contribution of Black Grandparents." *International Journal of Sociology of the Family* 23 (1993): 59–76.

UHLENBERG, PETER. "Population Aging and Social Policy." *Annual Review of Sociology* 18 (1992): 429–474.

WESTHEIMER, RUTH. *All in a Lifetime: An Autobiography by Ruth K. Westheimer* (New York: Warner Books, 1987).

——— and STEVEN KAPLAN. *Surviving Salvation: The Ethiopian Jewish Family in Transition* (New York: New York University Press, 1991).

——— and PIERRE LEHU. *Dr. Ruth Talks about Grandparents: Advice for Kids on Making the Most of a Special Relationship* (New York: Farrar, Straus & Giroux, 1997).

——— and BEN VAGODA. *The Value of Family: A Blueprint for the 21st Century* (New York: Warner Books, 1996).

Woolfson, Peter. "The Aging Franco-American and the Impact of Acculturation." *Ethnic Groups* 8 (1990): 181–199.